Linn's Philatelic Gems 3

Stampdom's fascinating rarities cover the length and breadth of the world, from a tiny island in the South Pacific to the mountains of Russian Georgia. *Philatelic Gems 3*, like its predecessor *Philatelic Gems 2*, presents the seldom-told stories of many of philately's lesser-known rarities. A few of these are even rarer than some detailed in the first *Philatelic Gems*.

Welcome to the continuing romance and mystery of *Philatelic Gems 3*.

by
Donna O'Keefe

Published by *Linn's Stamp News*, the world's largest and most informative stamp newspaper, Post Office Box 29, Sidney, Ohio 45365. *Linn's* is a division of Amos Press, Inc., which also publishes *Scott* catalogs and publications; *Coin World*, a weekly newspaper for the numismatic field; *Cars & Parts*, a monthly magazine for auto enthusiasts; and other publications for the stamp, coin and auto hobbies.
Second Printing
Copyright 1989 by Amos Press Inc.

400082   ISBN 0-940403-02-1

In Grateful Appreciation . . .

I wish to thank these collectors and dealers who helped make *Philatelic Gems 3* a reality:

Dr. Joseph Agris
Robert Ausubel
Alan Benjamin
Dr. Werner Bohne
John R. Boker, Jr.
Robert Cunliffe
Werner Elias
David Feldman
Keith Harmer
Leonard H. Hartmann
Bruce Hecht
George Holschauer
Virginia Horn
Susan Hughes
Heinz Katcher
Patricia Kaufmann
Robson Lowe
Walter Mader
Nancy Martin
Deb November
Peter Robertson
Robert A. Siegel
Mike Street
Herbert A. Trenchard
Scott Trepel
L.N. Williams

Donna O'Keefe

Contents

Introduction

What makes a stamp or cover a gem? How does it achieve this mark of philatelic greatness?

For some stamps, it is their uniqueness. A postmaster in Linz, Austria, carefully inserted a "9" on a stamp which was missing a value. This stamp is the only recorded copy with the manuscript "9." The postmaster unknowingly created a gem.

Another one-of-a-kind rarity comes from the West African nation of Cameroon. A printer for the British occupation forces created a unique provisional when he accidentally doubled the surcharge and inverted the letter "s" on the same stamp. Only one such stamp was produced. No price can be established for this gem because it is in the Royal Collection in England and is unlikely ever to be on the market.

Other gems are more common. They owe their status to their striking appearance and popularity. A Western Australia 2-penny stamp of 1879 has been discovered in lilac instead of yellow, the appropriate shade for that stamp. Mint copies of this shocking error bring five-figure realizations when they are sold.

Another rarity which immediately catches the eye of the collector is Britain's "B-blank" error. The check letter "A" is missing from the lower right-hand corner of the stamp. Several copies of this error have been discovered, but it is a gem nonetheless.

The fascinating stories behind the stamps often classify them as gems. Every gem must have an interesting story.

A scandalous postmistress in the Cayman Islands created numerous surcharged issues — some necessary, others not. These surcharges ruined the philatelic reputation of the Caymans for many years, but a few of these surcharged issues are true gems.

A shipment of stamps fell overboard and led to the release of one of Africa's greatest rarities. To replace this supply, a British Central Africa postmaster produced provisional stamps from narrow strips of paper used to indicate tax on checks. An inverted-center error from this issue is one of the world's most unusual gems.

Most of these rarities were issued in the 19th century, leading collectors to believe that a stamp must be old to be a gem. But several modern rarities exist. Only one pane of 50 of a Canal Zone Official with an inverted overprint survived. The pane has since been broken up. These inverted overprints are scarce.

The Swiss printer, Courvoisier, created two errors of color — one from the Channel Island of Jersey and the other from Isle of Man. These also can be classified as modern gems. The Jersey error was produced in 1969; the Manx error in 1974.

From Ireland comes a stunning missing-color error. With the missing silver inscription, the stamp — a 1976 issue honoring the United States bicentennial — appears to be a U.S. Albany essay.

Each of these stamps is a gem in its own right. This third edition of *Philatelic Gems* introduces collectors to many rare, yet underrated, stamps and covers. Their seldom-told stories will entice collectors, keeping the hope alive that someday — in that forgotten trunk in the attic, in great-grandfather's dusty album, or even at the local post office — a philatelic gem will be found.

'9' By Hand

VALUE: $18,700

Austria's rare 9-kreuzer stamp with the value inserted in manuscript.

Was it the diligence of a postmaster or the persistence of a customer that was responsible for one of Austria's most unusual rarities? Austria was the 12th country to issue adhesive stamps. Its first issue made its debut June 1, 1850. The design features the Austrian coat of arms with "KKPOST-STEMPEL" above and the denomination below.

The set consisted of 1-kreuzer, 2kr, 3kr, 6kr and 9kr denominations. The 9kr, however, was an afterthought necessitated by a change in postal rates.

The Austrian Government Printing Office printed the stamps in plates of 64 cliches of soft type metal. The original dies were produced without the value, which was inserted in the secondary dies.

The 9kr was the exception to this, according to Edwin Mueller in *Mercury Stamp Journal*. He said this stamp was produced from a plate of the 6kr. The "6" was removed and the "9" inserted in each cliche.

This resulted in different types. According to Scott catalog, on type I, the top of the "9" is about level with "KREUZER" and not near the top of the label. Type IA is similar to type I, but with 1¼ millimeters of spacing between "9" and "KREUZER," instead of ½mm. In type II, the top of "9" is much higher than the top of the word "KREUZER" and nearly touches the top of the label.

Because of these types, more rarities exist among the 9kr than among any of the other values in this issue. But one rarity stands out above the rest. It is unique.

During the printing of the 9kr, at least one copy slipped through without having the value printed on it. Mueller says this was a printing flaw, not a plate flaw. When a Linz, Austria, postmaster tried to sell a customer a 9kr stamp, he noticed that the stamp had no value.

It is not known whether the postmaster was conscientious or if the customer complained about paying for a non-denominated stamp. What is known is that the postmaster carefully inserted the "9" by hand in ink.

The customer, unaware that the true value of this stamp would someday be over a thousand times greater than its 9kr face value, licked it and stuck it to his letter. The stamp bears a Linz cancellation. This is the only example to have been found.

Austria's first issue was printed on paper watermarked "K K H M" (Kaiserlich-Koenigliches Handels-Ministerium, which translates Imperial and Royal Ministry of Commerce). The watermark ran vertically up the middle of each sheet, so only a few of the stamps at the edge of the panes bear any of the watermark.

The stamp with the manuscript "9" bears a large portion of the watermark on the right. Therefore, Mueller said the rarity is either from position 48 in the upper left pane or 24 in the lower left pane.

The stamp was in the Fitch and Levitt J. Bulkley collections, and later was bought by Charles Robertson of Bath, England. When the Robertson collection was sold by Harmers of London on June 22, 1983, the stamp realized £6,000. Cherrystone Stamp Company sold this rarity at its January 8-9, 1986, auction for $18,700, including the 10-percent buyer's premium.

A Blue Britannia

VALUE: $11,550

The rare Barbados Britannia 1-shilling blue error of color of 1863.

The old saying, "it pays to know people in high places," holds true for those early collectors lucky enough to obtain copies of the rare Barbados 1-shilling blue error of color.

Postal officials in Barbados adopted the same design for their first stamps as was used for Trinidad's first issue. This design features an allegoric figure of Britannia seated on bales of merchandise. She holds a spear in her right hand; her left hand rests on a shield. A ship is shown in the background at right. In each of the four corners of the stamp is a square white block featuring an eight-rayed star with a white dot in the center.

The first stamps of Barbados showed the name of the island at the bottom with no indication of denomination. The colors denoted the value. However, this proved impractical, and in 1859, Barbados began replacing these non-denominated stamps with those featuring values.

The same designs were employed, but "BARBADOS" was moved to the top of the stamp. The value was placed at the bottom. The non-denominated and denominated stamps were used simultaneously.

The Seated Britannia design again was used for the 1/- stamp introduced as part of the 1861 series. This denomination normally was printed in black.

In 1863, the printer, Perkins, Bacon & Company in England, shipped 500,000 copies of the stamp to the island. When the supply arrived, postal officials inspected the stamps and discovered they were printed in blue instead of black. The officials packed up the shipment and returned it to the printer — at least most of the shipment, that is.

A few of the blue color errors found their way into the hands of collectors. The stamps were never placed on sale. It is believed that a postal official shared a few of these color errors with his collector friends — for a profit, no doubt.

Only nine copies of the error exist. Each is marked in pen with a corner-to-corner cross, which has been cleaned off. None has been used. Scott catalog lists this error at $27,500. One copy was auctioned March 11, 1987, by Christie's/Robson Lowe as part of the Isleham collection. It realized $11,550, including a 10-percent buyer's premium.

Imperf-Between Variety

VALUE: $15,000
*Vertical strip of three of
the 1/- imperf-between.*

Bermuda's 1894 1-shilling green was not issued until 14 years after it was produced. This issue then was found to include a major error. The 1/- was part of the 1882-1903 series. For some unknown reason, the 3-penny, 6d and 1/- values were produced in 1880 but

13

were not released for several years.

The 3d was the first to be placed into use. It was issued in 1882. The 1/- went on sale in 1894. Twenty-three years passed before the 6d was issued.

Although the design for these values was the same as the 1865-74 issue, the 1882-1903 stamps differed in that they featured compound perforations, 14 by 12½, instead of perf 14. The stamps were typographed in sheets of 240 (four panes of 60). Only 24,000 of the 1/- were issued.

The gems of the 1/- are the imperforate-between vertical strips. In *The Postal History and Stamps of Bermuda*, M.H. Ludington says two rows of perfs were missing between the eighth and ninth, and ninth and last rows of each pane, probably on the same sheet. So, at least 24 strips of this error must have existed.

Ludington recorded an irregular block of five, two strips of four, eight strips of three and a pair with the interpane at the bottom. These copies all are unused. A pair canceled at Ireland Island on January 3, 1897, exists, as does a used single canceled at Hamilton. Harmers of London sold two vertical strips of three of the imperf-between variety at its January 2, 1968, auction. The Scott catalog lists vertical strips of three at $15,000.

A copy of the 1/- green also exists imperf vertically. This is recorded in both Ludington's book and Robson Lowe's *The Encyclopaedia of British Empire Postage Stamps: North America*. It is not listed in Scott or Gibbons catalogs. The stamp is perf 14 at top and bottom, 12½ on the left side, with the right side being imperf with a wide margin.

Ludington says that since the stamp does not exist with wing margins, and since this variety contains portions of the watermarked inscription, the stamp comes from the last vertical row of probably one sheet only. Thus, 20 stamps existed.

Topsy-Turvy Tree

VALUE: $4,400

*British Central Africa's 1898 1-penny
provisional with the center inverted.*

A lost shipment of stamps led to the release of one of the world's most unusual provisionals and one of Africa's greatest rarities. In 1897, a supply of stamps was ordered for British Central Africa, which was under charter to the British South Africa Company.

The stamps arrived at the coast of Africa from the London printer on schedule. The shipment then had to be transported up the

Zambezi River by barge.

Upon arrival, postal officials discovered the stamps had disappeared. Apparently, they had fallen overboard sometime during the journey.

The postal officials immediately ordered a new supply from London, but the colony was experiencing a shortage of 1-penny stamps. The new stamps would not arrive in time. The postmaster, J.T. Gosling, ordered the surcharging of the colony's 3-shilling stamps. Each was surcharged "ONE/PENNY" in red.

However, this was only a temporary solution. Speculators bought up large quantities of the provisional, creating another shortage. In March 1898, the postal officials created a new provisional — a most unusual stamp.

Since the post office now was running short of other values, none could be spared for surcharging. The innovative postmaster ordered the printing of narrow strips of paper with an impression used for stamping the tax on checks.

The emergency stamps consisted of a rectangular frame with the inscription "INTERNAL" at the top and "POSTAGE" below. These were printed in ultramarine. The center, printed in red, featured a tree (the arms of the colony) surrounded by the inscription "BRITISH CENTRAL AFRICA PROTECTORATE/ONE/PENNY." The stamps were printed in sheets of 30 (two horizontal rows of 15).

The ultramarine portion was printed first. The red check die impressions were then stamped one at a time. For such a tedious process, few errors occurred. Those that exist are great rarities.

The scarcest are those with the center inverted. Only 15 examples, all unused, have been recorded. These are listed in Scott catalog at $15,000. One was sold by Christie's/Robson Lowe in its March 11, 1987, auction as part of the Isleham collection. It realized $4,400, including a 10-percent buyer's premium. Stamps with a double oval catalog $2,750 used.

Another error, a pair with one stamp missing the oval, is priced in Scott at $10,000 unused. A pair with three ovals is unpriced.

The provisional stamps made their debut March 11. To prevent speculation, the postmaster ordered that the stamps were not to be sold to the general public. They were to be affixed to correspondence only by the postal clerk. To guard against forgeries, he initialed the first 16 sheets (480) stamps "JG" or "JTG." Initialed copies are listed in Scott at $800 used.

This was tedious. Gosling eventually gave up and ordered the remainder to be printed on the back with an uninked type. This type featured various combinations of figures and letters. These make it possible to reconstruct the sheets, since the stamps were numbered right to left from 1 to 15 and 16 to 30. The letters follow no order, and no two stamps show the same combination.

The first stamps were issued imperforate, and it is this issue which includes the errors. In mid-1898, a new supply of the emergency issue was created with the same check stamp design, but this time perforated 12. The frame was printed in blue.

Error in Stamp Design

VALUE: $35,750

A unique strip of four of the British Guiana Patimus issue appears on this entire letter to Georgetown, British Guiana, from Plantation Spartar.

British Guiana's 1852 set of stamps not only ranks among the rarest stamps of the world but also rates as one of the most expensive issues showing an error in design. The 1¢ magenta and 4¢ blue feature a ship and the motto of the colony.

The motto is "Damus petimus que vicissim" (We give and we seek in turn). However, the designer misspelled the second word "patimus." The error is so famous that collectors refer to this set as the Patimus issue.

These stamps are scarce, particularly in unused condition, as their catalog values reflect. Scott catalog lists the 1¢ at $12,500 unused and $6,500 used, and the 4¢ at $15,000 unused and $6,500 used. But despite their scarcity, these stamps are overshadowed by their more famous sisters — the British Guiana 1¢ magenta, the "world's most valuable stamp," and the colony's first issue, the Cottonreels.

Even as an error in stamp design, the "Post Office" Mauritius stamps would be considered the scarcest and most expensive.

Yet, the British Guiana 1852 1¢ and 4¢ are indeed gems of philately. The 1¢ covered the rate for newspapers; the 4¢ for ½-ounce inland letters. The 1852 set, lithographed in London by Waterlow, was a vast improvement over the colony's first issue, the crudely printed Cottonreels which had been produced locally.

Waterlow engraved pairs of each denomination, creating two types. Lithographic stones then were produced from these engravings. The stamps are printed on fragile, easily damaged surface-

VALUE: $15,000
A scarce unused copy of the 4¢ Patimus issue was owned by Ferrari.

printed paper, contributing to the scarcity of this issue. Few copies have survived.

Count Ferrari, the famous French collector, owned an unused copy of the 4¢ and a block of four of the 1¢, as well as used examples of both. Alfred Caspary bought these stamps at the Ferrari sales in the early 1900s.

David Feldman sold the block of four of the 1¢, used on a fragment, at his November 19-23, 1985, auction in New York City. It realized $14,950, including a 15-percent buyer's premium. At its May 27, 1986, AMERIPEX '86 auction, Stanley Gibbons Auctions sold a unique strip of four on an entire letter to Georgetown from Plantation Spartar. It realized $35,750, including a 10-percent buyer's premium.

Reprints of the 1852 1¢ and 4¢ also exist. They can be identified by their thicker paper. Also, the colors are much brighter. The reprints exist perforated 12½ or imperforate.

Only One Survivor

VALUE: $50,000
The only known vertical tete-beche pair of the Buenos Aires 1859 1 peso.

Only two pairs of the Buenos Aires 1859 1-peso tete-beche pair have been recorded. The whereabouts of only one of these pairs is known today.

Buenos Aires, now the capital of Argentina, issued its own stamps as a province in 1858 and 1859. These issues featured a common design showing a paddle-wheel steamship.

The scarcest of these stamps are the 1859 1p tete-beche pairs. In tete-beche pairs, one stamp is in the normal, upright position; the other is upside down. While preparing the plate for the 1p stamp, the printer turned the first cliche in the fifth row upside down. This produced the tete-beche varieties. Scott catalog lists these varieties at $50,000.

Count Phillippe von Ferrari owned a horizontal tete-beche pair of the Buenos Aires 1p. When the Ferrari collections were auctioned in France following World War I, American collector Alfred Lichtenstein bought the pair. The present whereabouts of this rare item is unknown.

A vertical tete-beche pair was discovered in Germany. Another American collector, Alfred Caspary, purchased this pair. When Caspary's collection was sold by H.R. Harmer of New York in 1958, Lars Amundsen paid $1,700 to add it to his collection. John R. Boker Jr. later purchased this item to complete his collection of Buenos Aires. This pair now is owned by a collector who wishes to remain anonymous.

Another copy of the 1p has been recorded which has a portion of the adjoining stamp in the reversed or tete-beche position. The present whereabouts of this copy also is unknown.

Doubled and Inverted

VALUE: Indeterminable

The unique Cameroon 3/- on 3m stamp with double surcharge and inverted "s" is in the Royal Collection.

A unique surcharge variety of the West African nation of Cameroon resides in the Royal Collection in Buckingham Palace. In 1884, Germany established a protectorate called Kamerun. Stamps of the German Empire were overprinted "Kamerun" in 1897. In 1900, Germany printed stamps inscribed "Kamerun" especially for the protectorate. These feature the familiar German colonial designs depicting the kaiser's yacht, *Hohenzollern*. These stamps still were in circulation when World War I broke out in 1914.

That same year British and French forces invaded Cameroon. The British occupied the German capital of Duala but found no trace of postage stamps.

For a time, letters sent from Cameroon were inscribed "No Stamps Available." Later, the British captured the West African liner *Professor Woermann* in the harbor of Freetown, Sierra Leone. When they boarded the vessel, they found a supply of Yacht stamps addressed to the postmaster of Cameroon.

The British overprinted these with the initials "C.E.F" (Cameroons Expeditionary Force) and surcharged them with new values. These stamps saw provisional use on mail from Cameroon and were used for a time by both the British and the French.

The pfennig denominations were surcharged with pence values. The mark denominations were surcharged with the same numeral values as appeared on the original stamps but with an "s" representing "shilling." The overprints and surcharges were applied in blue or black.

The shilling surcharges were applied from a single setting, with only the numerals changing. In his effort to produce the provisionals as quickly as possible, the printer mistakenly inverted the "s" in the setting for stamp No. 12 in the sheet of 20. Each shilling value, therefore, exists with an inverted "s" variety. Scott catalog lists these varieties each at $1,000 unused and $1,500 used.

But the printer made another mistake — one which would create one of the world's rarest stamps. One sheet of 20 of the 3/- on 3m denomination received a double surcharge. Stamps with the double surcharge are scarce, cataloging at $5,000 mint.

But the great rarity is stamp No. 12 from that sheet. It not only has the double surcharge, but also the inverted "s." Since only one sheet received the double surcharge and only one position on the sheet had the inverted "s," this stamp is unique.

Catalogs which list this stamp decline to price it, for obvious reasons. If it were sold, would it rival the British Guiana 1¢ magenta as the world's most expensive stamp? That question probably will never be answered. The Cameroon rarity is in the Royal Collection, and it is highly unlikely the stamp will ever be offered for sale.

Lost to the Sea

VALUE: $8,900
Only four mint copies exist of Canada's London-to-London semiofficial.

Canada and her provinces are well-known for their scarce airmail stamps. Among the scarcest is a semiofficial issued for a fatal London-to-London flight. In 1927, the Carling Breweries of London, Ontario, sponsored a publicity contest challenging aviators to make the 3,900-mile non-stop trip from London, Ontario, to London, England.

The company offered $25,000 for the successful completion of the trip by a Canadian or British pilot. According to L. Seale Holmes in his *Philatelic Catalogue of Canada and British North America*, Carling Breweries appointed a secret committee to select the pilot.

The committee chose Captain Terrence Tully and his navigator Lieutenant James Medcalf.

A special semiofficial stamp was issued for the flight with the permission of the Canadian government. This 25¢ stamp features portraits of Tully and Medcalf with their plane, *Sir John Carling*, flying over a globe. Only 100 stamps were produced by a printer in London, Ontario. The Canadian Post Office sent an inspector to oversee the production.

This issue was given only to those closely connected with the flight. Most of the stamps were used on mail carried on the plane, says Holmes.

The *Sir John Carling* first took off from London, Ontario, on August 29, 1927. The mail was postmarked and placed on the plane. Bad weather forced the plane to return to London. Another attempt was made September 1, but again the plane was forced down because of unfavorable weather.

By this time, another two planes were attempting to make the flight to England. A contest developed between the three planes. *Sir John Carling* flew from London to St. John's, Newfoundland, on September 5. On September 6, the pilots received word that one of the other planes, *Old Glory*, sponsored by Herst Newspapers, had taken off for England. Tully and Medcalf immediately loaded their plane and took off, trying to beat their competitor.

Although naval units closely watched the progress of the planes, both planes vanished. Wreckage of *Old Glory* eventually was found at sea. No trace of *Sir John Carling* was found. The flight of the third plane was aborted.

Along with the *Sir John Carling,* all but one cover bearing the London-to-London stamps vanished. This cover belonged to the postmaster of London, Ontario. It was removed from the mailbag on one of the earlier aborted flights.

Four mint copies of the stamp exist. One was auctioned by J.N. Sissons, Inc., in Toronto on January 14, 1986. It realized $5,750. Harmers of London sold a copy for £6,325 (about $8,900) at its March 11-12, 1986, "Pegasus" collection auction.

Compound Overprint Varieties

VALUE: $5,000

A "CANAL ZONE" inverted overprint
on a Panama 2¢ inverted-center error.

Although many errors and varieties exist on the Canal Zone's early overprinted issues, a few stand out above the rest. The Canal Zone began issuing stamps in 1904 when the United States assumed jurisdiction.

It was not until 1928 that a regular issue was printed specifically for the Canal Zone. Until then, stamps of Panama and the U.S. were overprinted for use in the Zone.

As is typical with overprints, many varieties exist. Double overprints, overprints in different styles of type, and missing and inverted overprints are some of the varieties which attract collectors to these issues. Several of these are rarities.

Inverts exist among the first overprinted issue. One of the 2¢ rarities has the "CANAL ZONE" overprint doubled and inverted. According to *Canal Zone Stamps* by Gilbert N. Plass, Geoffrey Brewster and Richard H. Salz, one pane of the 2¢ was overprinted with "CANAL ZONE" inverted. Only one stamp exists with the overprint both doubled and inverted. It catalogs in Scott at $4,000.

Another 2¢ rarity features not only the variety "PANAMA" reading down at left and up at right, but also with "CANAL ZONE" inverted. This variety catalogs at $3,500 unused or used.

The gem of the 5¢ value of the first issue is the pair with one stamp missing the "CANAL ZONE" overprint. Only four examples exist. Two are the right top and bottom stamps in an unused block of six. One is the top center stamp of another unused block of six. Another is the center stamp in a vertical strip on cover. Scott catalog lists these at $2,250 unused or used.

A similar error occurs on the 10¢ of the first issue. One is part of a block of four. Another is contained in a block of six. Both blocks are unused. The third copy of the error is the middle stamp in a used strip of four. Scott catalogs this variety at $2,750 unused or used.

Another rarity of the 10¢ features "CANAL ZONE" doubled. Only two copies have been recorded, according to *Canal Zone Stamps*. Both are used. They catalog at $3,000.

Two different styles of types — antique and regular — were used for the 1904-06 series of overprints on Panama stamps. The rarities among these are the 1¢ with the overprint inverted, and the same denomination with a double overprint. It is believed a pane of 100 inverts was created.

Collectors failed to notice the invert variety until several years after the overprint's release. As a result, most copies of the inverted overprint varieties were used as postage. Only six copies have been recorded. Of course, since most copies were used, there is a chance that examples may some day be found in forgotten correspondence.

The pane of the double overprints also went undetected by collectors. *Canal Zone Stamps* reports that 20 examples have been recorded. The 10 unused copies were not discovered until 1969, so there still is hope for collectors. Scott lists the inverted overprint at $2,000, and double overprints at $1,200 unused and $800 used.

Varieties plagued the 8¢-on-50¢ overprinted and surcharged issue of the 1904-06 series. The most notable is the rose-brown overprint with "8" omitted.

Only six examples exist. According to *Canal Zone Stamps*, one was due to either a paper fold or foreign matter coming between the type and the stamp. The other copies were created by a horizontally shifted surcharge. Scott lists this variety at $3,500 unused.

The 1905 8¢-on-50¢ surcharge exists with "PANAMA" reading down and up. It catalogs at $3,250 unused and used.

The printer created a true gem in the 1906-07 series. He applied the overprint to Panama's Fernandez de Cordoba 2¢ carmine red and black. However, he did not realize that copies of the stamp had the center inverted. This error was compounded when the printer applied the overprint upside down, reading up.

Only nine copies have been recorded of this error — one of the Canal Zone's greatest rarities. One copy exists on cover. No unused examples have been discovered. Scott catalog lists this rarity at $5,000. An example of this error realized $2,800 at the October 31-November 2, 1986, auction conducted by Jacques C. Schiff, Inc.

Other spectacular errors in this series are the 2¢ and 5¢ stamps overprinted "ZONE CANAL" and those overprinted "CANAL" only. Only two copies of the 5¢ "ZONE CANAL" and three of the 5¢ "CANAL" errors have been discovered. No used copies exist of either value.

Scott prices the "ZONE CANAL" varieties at $2,000 for the 2¢ and $2,750 for the 5¢. The "CANAL"-only error is listed at $1,750. The "ZONE" must be completely omitted for this stamp to be considered the scarce variety.

The 1909 10¢ issue exists in horizontal and vertical pairs with the overprint omitted on one stamp of each pair. The authors of *Canal Zone Stamps* say this was the result of one pane of the 10¢ receiving the overprint at a slight angle. Three stamps in this pane did not receive the overprint.

Two horizontal and one vertical pair exist. Scott lists the horizontal pairs at $3,000 and the vertical pair at $3,500.

Another Panama inverted-center error was overprinted as part of the 1909-10 series, creating another spectacular rarity for the Canal Zone. George Wirth discovered this 1¢ gem in 1932. It was removed from a postcard and was canceled in 1913.

The second copy did not turn up until the 1950s. The clipped perforations at the left indicate that it was part of a handmade booklet. Only two other copies have been recorded. All are used. Scott prices these rarities at $11,000. Only 10 copies have been discovered of the 1909-10 8¢ in a vertical pair with one stamp missing the overprint. It catalogs at $1,500.

A compound variety appears on the 2¢ of the 1912-16 series. The stamp features an inverted center and inverted overprint reading down. The error exists unused and used, and in panes used for homemade booklets. It catalogs in Scott at $5,000.

Two booklet panes of six of the 2¢ in the 1918-20 series have been discovered with the overprint omitted on the left vertical row of three stamps. This error catalogs at $2,250.

Gems of the 1920-21 series are a vertical pair of the 1¢ with the overprint missing on one stamp, and the 2¢ with "CANAL" missing. Scott lists these at $2,000 and $3,000, respectively. Both are found unused only.

In 1924, stamps of the U.S. were overprinted for the Canal Zone. The 12¢ of the 1924-25 series exists with "ZONE" inverted. "CANAL" appears upright.

A similar error occurred on the 1¢ of this series, but it was detected at the post office. The 12¢ wasn't discovered until 1926. Only two unused and seven used copies have been recorded. Scott lists this error at $3,000 unused and $2,000 used.

The 3¢, 5¢, 10¢, 12¢ and 15¢ of the 1925-26 series exist with the overprint variety "ZONE/ZONE." These catalog between $500 and $3,500. The 5¢, 10¢, 15¢ and 17¢ exist with the overprint "ZONE" only. These catalog between $900 and $3,500. "CANAL" only varieties also exist. The 5¢ is known in a horizontal pair with one stamp missing the overprint. This catalogs at $3,000.

Several 20¢ rarities exist in this series, including "CANAL" inverted, "ZONE" inverted, and the variety "ZONE/CANAL." Scott lists each of these at $3,500.

The Accepted CTO

VALUE: $1,100 plus

Bottom half of the only surviving pane of the Canal Zone 1947 6¢ Official stamps with inverted overprints. This pane has since been broken up.

Seldom is a canceled-to-order (CTO) item considered a rarity, but such an item from the Canal Zone qualifies as a "philatelic gem." This issue is an airmail Official stamp with the overprint inverted.

In 1941, the Canal Zone Post Office ordered the overprinting of several of its regular and airmail stamps to create Official issues. These stamps replaced the Official stamps bearing the perforated letter "P." The post office felt the overprinted stamps would be easier for postal employees to recognize, making it easier to detect misuse of these stamps.

The overprint reads, "Official Panama Canal." Two types of this overprint exist. One is printed in two lines; the other in three.

Use of these Officials was restricted to government departments. At first, the post office refused to sell these overprinted Officials to collectors, but later relented. It agreed to sell the stamps, but only after they were canceled.

According to Gilbert N. Plass, Geoffrey Brewster and Richard H. Salz in *Canal Zone Stamps*, Director of Posts C.H. Calhoun justified this decision by saying, "The speculation in these stamps reached a point where they were eventually forged as to overprints, and it was apparently a situation that approximated a monopoly."

While the opportunity to purchase these previously unobtainable Officials delighted some collectors, others shunned the CTOs. Rollin E. Flower, who was then president of the American Philatelic Society, wrote to the postmaster general of the United States to protest this action. On the other hand, the American Stamp Dealers' Association and American Air Mail Society congratulated the Canal Zone on its decision.

The Officials were canceled with a marking which reads, "Balboa Heights, Canal Zone" between two wavy lines.

No one suspected when these CTOS were first released that one day a rarity would exist among them. In 1947, during the overprinting of the 6¢ Gaillard Cut airmail stamp for official use, the printer created what was to become one of the Canal Zone's major rarities. Thirty-two panes of 50 of the 6¢ stamps were inserted into the press upside down, resulting in an inverted overprint.

During the inspection, 31 panes were discovered and destroyed. But one escaped detection. According to *Canal Zone Stamps*, this pane apparently was sent to the Canal Zone Philatelic Agency for stock, since all copies are canceled with the special roller cancel that was then used on all Official stamps sold to the public.

The pane was the lower-left pane with straight edges at the top and right. Only 36 of the inverts are perforated on four sides, 13 have one straight edge, and one has two straight edges. Only the top two horizontal rows (10 stamps) had the roller cancel inverted.

Canal Zone Stamps further states that according to prominent U.S. collector George W. Brett, Judge E.I.P. Tatelman, a Canal Zone magistrate, discovered the inverted overprinted stamps in a group of panes he purchased from the Balboa Heights Postmaster Charles Hinz. Guarding his reputation, Hinz vehemently denied leaking the pane to the judge.

The Scott U.S. Specialized catalog lists a single used copy at $1,100. Many collectors thumb their noses at CTOs since these stamps are canceled specifically for collectors without having passed through the mails. But Canal Zone collectors overlook their prejudices when it comes to this gem.

The Scandalous Postmistress

VALUE: $19,550

The Cayman Islands rare 1907-08 ½-penny-on-5/- pair with the surcharge omitted on the right-hand stamp.

A philatelic scandal resulted from the surcharging of early issues of the Cayman Islands. And, oddly enough, the Caymans' greatest rarities are among these surcharged issues.

Since provisional issues were subject to considerable speculation in the late 1800s, Lord Ripon, the secretary of state for the British colonies, handed down an order in 1893 concerning the surcharging of postage stamps. It stated:

"If proper care is taken to maintain a sufficient supply of stamps, the practice of surcharging is unnecessary, and it should never be resorted to unless absolutely required for the convenience of the public, and in every case the officer responsible for keeping up the supply of stamps should be liable to be fined."

The Cayman Islands, located in the Caribbean Sea, issued its first stamps in 1900, and for seven years, followed a conservative issuing policy. But when the islands sinned by releasing provisionals, they drew the wrath of the philatelic world.

In 1906, a law was passed requiring revenue tax to be paid on certain documents. This tax was to be paid by affixing postage stamps. To meet these rates, a new set of bicolored stamps, in denominations of 4 pence, 6d, 1-shilling and 5/-, was released March 13, 1907. At the same time, a new supply of the monocolored ½d, 1d and 2½d stamps was sent to the islands.

The Caymans were a dependency of Jamaica. The governor of Jamaica ordered the withdrawal of all older stamps to be replaced by the new set of bicolored stamps. However, the Caymans postmistress, Gwendolyn A. Parsons, took the order literally and withdrew all stamps except the bicolored set. The withdrawn issues included the new supply of the monocolored ½d, 1d and 2½d.

Needless to say, it wasn't long before the islanders experienced a severe shortage of low-value stamps. On June 11, 1907, G.S.S. Hirst, the Caymans commissioner, wrote to the governor of Jamaica requesting a provisional issue of ½d stamps to meet the islands' needs.

The request was reluctantly granted, but the commissioner was instructed that these provisionals were for postal use only and could not be sold to stamp dealers. A supply of 1d stamps was surcharged "One/Halfpenny" in Jamaica and sent to the Caymans. No major errors or varieties exist on this provisional.

By using the 1d stamps to produce a provisional, the postal authorities created another shortage — this time of the 1d values. The commissioner took it upon his own to issue provisionals without the permission of the Jamaican authorities.

A crude surcharging device was created by inserting two pieces of metal type into a wooden handle. Miss Parsons, the postmistress, surcharged the new 5/- bicolored stamp with a "1D" value. A double surcharge exists which is listed in Scott catalog at $17,500.

Surcharging stamps became an easy method of solving stamp shortages on the Caymans. To create a new supply of ½d stamps, Miss Parsons surcharged sheets of the 5/- bicolored issues with a device featuring a "1" over a "2" (no fraction bar) with a "D" to the right. Numerous errors occurred on this provisional. Some are extremely rare.

Stamps with an inverted surcharge catalog at $20,000. Those with a double surcharge are listed in Scott at $15,000 mint and $16,500 used. A double surcharge with one inverted exists. Scott does not price this error.

Extremely scarce is a pair of the ½d on 5/- with the surcharge omitted on one of the stamps. While Scott lists this at $30,000, a pair sold in the November 19-23, 1985, David Feldman auction in New York for $19,550, including a 15-percent buyer's premium.

Another provisional was produced by Miss Parsons in 1908. The luxury yacht, *Zenaida,* called at Georgetown unexpectedly and offered to carry mail to Cuba. The islanders saw this as an opportunity to send mail to the United States without waiting for the regular dispatch of mail, which was not due until the end of the month.

However, 2½d stamps were needed to meet the rate, and once again the islands experienced a shortage. So Miss Parsons began surcharging 4d bicolored stamps with a 2½d surcharge, again without the fraction bar. The normal surcharge is listed in Scott catalog at $3,850 mint and $5,000 used. Copies with the double surcharge are priced at $35,000 mint. Harmers of New York sold a copy of the normal surcharge for $1,265, including a 10-percent buyer's premium, at its January 28-29, 1987, sale.

The creation of provisionals did not stop there. Miss Parson became obsessed with creating her own stamps. In 1908, she produced provisional stamped envelopes by handstamping them "Postage Paid." Postal cards and envelopes also were marked "Paid ¼d."

By this time, collectors were up in arms. The philatelic press condemned the Caymans for its prolific surcharged issues. The British government demanded an investigation. But Miss Parsons and the commissioner were cleared of all charges since they had not made a profit on the sale of the provisionals. They were absolved of their sins, but the philatelic reputation of the Caymans was besmirched for many years to come.

Spice Island Gems

VALUE: $6,500

*An unused example of Ceylon's rare
first issue, the 6-penny plum of 1857.*

The 1857-59 4-penny and 9d stamps have long been recognized as the gems of the spice island of Ceylon (present day Sri Lanka). Frequently forgotten, however, is the 6d of 1857, Ceylon's first postage stamp.

Penny postage was introduced in Ceylon in 1856. A law was passed requiring that postage be prepaid with stamps. Since Ceylon had no stamps, a supply was ordered from the British printer Perkins, Bacon & Company.

De La Rue & Company in London also was asked to print ½d stamps and envelopes.

William Humphreys engraved a portrait of Queen Victoria by Edward Henry Corbould for use on the 1d, 2d, 5d, 6d, 10d and 1-shilling stamps. The 4d, 8d, 9d, 1/9d and 2d featured a portrait of the queen engraved by Charles Henry Jeens for the stamps of the

Ionian Islands and the frame used for the 6d of Tasmania.

Perkins, Bacon printed the stamps in sheets of 240, imperforate. The 1d blue and 6d plum were printed on both blued paper and white paper. The other values were printed on white paper.

The 6d was the first stamp to be printed, and supplies immediately were sent to Ceylon. They arrived in time for the stamp to be issued April 1, 1857, the day the new postal rate went into effect. Other values followed later in April.

Although it is unlikely the 6d will ever gain the recognition given to the 4d and 9d of this series, the stamp is scarce nonetheless, particularly in unused condition. Scott catalog lists the stamp at $12,500 unused and $725 used. An unused example sold at the January 30, 1986, Colonial Stamp Company auction for $6,500, including a 10-percent buyer's premium.

Examples of the 6d, as well as the famous 4d, were part of the extensive collection of Baron Anthony de Worms. De Worms had a monopoly on the stamps of Ceylon for many years. His family owned coffee estates on the island, so the island's stamps were easily accessible to him. It was not until his collection was dispersed in 1938 that many of these Ceylon rarities became available on the philatelic market.

A Tattered Rarity

VALUE: $7,000

Only one example of the Chile 1910 invert error has ever been found.

In 1955, a collector purchased a tattered copy of Chile's 1910 1-centavo Independence Centenary stamp from a Chilean railroad employee. The collector paid 500 pesos for the stamp, an unusually high sum for this issue, particularly for a defective copy.

But this stamp is special. The center is printed upside down. And this is the only copy known to exist.

Noted philatelic writer L.N. Williams says the collector submitted the stamp for expertization, and it was found to be genuine. The expertizer also mentioned the stamp's many faults — small holes, creasing, and two perforations pulled.

The 1c is part of a set of 15 values issued in 1910 to commemorate the 100th anniversary of Chile's independence. The nine low values are horizontal in format and depict memorable events in the history of Chile. The six high values are vertical in format and reproduce monuments honoring Chile's leaders and heroes.

The inscription on the 1c says the stamp depicts the oath of independence. However, Williams says the design really shows the army of Argentine General San Martin entering Lima, the capital of Peru, in 1821. So, the stamp not only features an inverted center but an error in stamp design as well.

Contemporary philatelic accounts cited this issue as one of

Chile's most beautiful sets. The center of each is black; the frames appear in various colors.

The stamps were printed by the American Bank Note Company in New York. Since the frames and centers were printed separately, it can be assumed that a sheet was turned upside down during the second printing process. Do others exist?

The 1c inverted center was sold by Harmers of New York in 1971 for $4,000. It again was sold in 1984 by David Feldman in Geneva, Switzerland, for 41,400 Swiss francs. Scott catalog lists this unique stamp from Chile at $7,000.

An Upset Statesman

VALUE: $5,000

Chinese collectors refer to this $2 inverted center as an inverted frame.

Few stamp errors have sent printers scurrying across the ocean to buy back their mistakes. But the American Bank Note Company made such an effort when China's $2 Dr. Sun Yat-sen stamp of 1941 appeared with an inverted center.

In 1941, China ordered 16 denominations of stamps ranging from ½¢ to $20 to be printed by ABNC in New York. Each featured a portrait of Chinese statesman Dr. Sun Yat-sen. In 1945, China revised its postal rates and announced that the 1941 series would be withdrawn from sale November 30.

A few days before the withdrawal date, a high school student, Cheng Ching-chu, visited the post office in his hometown of Chungking. The post office was selling these stamps in bundles. Cheng bought one of the bundles. When he returned home, he discovered that Dr. Sun Yat-sen's head was upside down on one pane of 50 of the $2 stamp.

The discovery of this error, while delighting stamp collectors, irritated the Chinese, who felt it disrespectful to portray their beloved statesman upside down. Embarrassed by the error, the ABNC went to great lengths to recover the pane. The company advertised to buy back the pane, and even sent a representative to China to try to recover the inverts from Cheng. But to no avail. Cheng eventually broke up the pane into blocks and singles and sold them to other collectors.

Huang Kuang-sheng details the provenance of 29 copies of the invert in *Postal Service Today*, Number 306, the journal of the Taiwan Postal Service. The dollar denominations of the 1941 series were printed in two colors. The ABNC first printed the frames in one color, followed by the centers in a different color. During the second printing process, a sheet of the $2 stamps was turned upside down, resulting in the inverted centers.

Although it is the center that is inverted, some Chinese collectors feel it inappropriate to portray Dr. Sun Yat-sen upside down. They show the frame inverted.

The $2 stamp was printed in sheets of 300 and then cut into panes of 50. What happened to the remaining 250 stamps? It is likely the error was caught by the printer, and these 250 stamps were destroyed. But it is possible some may exist.

This invert has become one of the great rarities of China. Scott catalog lists it at $5,000 mint. Unlike its counterpart, the 1915 Hall of Classics invert, no used copies of the Sun Yat-sen error exist.

'50' Instead of '5'

VALUE: $10,450

The printer compounded his mistake on this rare "50"-instead-of-"5" error.

Several rarities exist among the first and second issues of Colombia. Known as the Grenadine Confederation at that time, Colombia issued its first stamps in 1859. The set consisted of 2½-centavo green, 5c blue, 5c violet, 10c red brown, 20c blue, 1-peso carmine and 1p rose. Celestino and Jeronimo Martinez lithographed the stamps from stones on which a matrix had been transferred 55 times (11 vertical and five horizontal rows). The stamps were printed imperforate on gummed paper.

The printers created tete-beche pairs of the 5c blue and 20c blue by turning a few of the transfers upside down. A tete-beche pair has one stamp inverted in relation to the other. Six positions on the 5c sheet had stamps turned upside down.

In the November 1951 *Collectors Club Journal*, F.G. Larsen discussed the first two issues of Colombia. He described the positions of the 5c inverted errrors as: ninth and 11th stamps in the first horizontal row; second stamp in the second horizontal row; eighth and 10th stamps in the fourth horizontal row; and sixth stamp in the fifth horizontal row. The 5c tete-beche pairs are listed in Scott catalog at $3,000 mint and $6,500 used.

Another spectacular error occurred with the printing of the 5c. A transfer of the 20c stamp was mistakenly made on the stone of the 5c. The printers tried to rectify the mistake by converting the "2" to a "5." Not only were they less than successful in making the "2" look like a "5," but they also forgot to remove the "0." This result-

VALUE: $27,500

This pair of the Colombian first issue shows the 20c together with the 5c error of transfer. The pair was in the Caspary and Ferrari collections.

ed in the scarce "50"-instead-of-"5" error. Only used copies exist. Scott lists the error at $8,500.

An example was auctioned March 12, 1987, by Christie's/Robson Lowe as part of the Isleham collection. It realized $10,450, including a 10-percent buyer's premium.

The printers later corrected their mistake by punching out the central portion of the design. Count Ferrari, the famous French collector, owned a portion of a sheet of the 5c Colombian stamps which contained three tete-beche pairs and the error 20c with the central portion punched.

The true gems of Colombia are the errors which occurred in the printing of the 20c of the first issue. Tete-beche pairs exist. Larsen said the error occurred on the second stamp in the second horizontal row. Scott catalog lists this error at $20,000 mint and used.

A transfer of the 5c also was made on the 20c. Copies of the 20c printed se-tenant with the 5c are extremely scarce. Only mint examples exist. Scott lists this error at $30,000.

Ferrari owned a se-tenant horizontal pair of the 20c and the 5c error of transfer. Before Ferrari purchased it, the pair was in the Larish and Castle collections. This pair was bought by Alfred Caspary. During the Caspary sales conducted by H.R. Harmer of New York in 1958, the pair realized $2,000. This pair also was auctioned March 12, 1987, by Christie's/Robson Lowe. It realized $27,500, including a 10-percent buyer's premium.

Caspary also bought Ferrari's 20c tete-beche pair. It realized $1,600 at the Caspary sales.

Saul Newbury owned a pair of the 20c with the 5c error of transfer partially corrected. Newbury bought this pair in 1924 in the Adler sale for $51. W.H. Crocker owned a block of nine of the 20c containing the 5c error of transfer. Newbury purchased this block when it was sold by Harmer Rooke & Company in London in 1939.

In 1860, the Colombian Post Office canceled its contract with the Martinez brothers and entered into a new contract with Daniel Ayala and Ignacio Medrano. Only one error of major significance occurred during the printing of the 1860 issue.

Tete-beche pairs exist of the 10c yellow buff. The error occurred on the second stamp in the second horizontal row. It was later corrected. Scott lists this error at $5,000 mint.

Stickers as Stamps

VALUE: Indeterminable

Only one Compania Colombiana stamp without the 10-centavo surcharge exists on cover. The cover was sent from Cartagena to Barranquilla.

Colombia's Compania Colombiana de Navegacion Aerea airmail stamps are among the most unusual in the world. Some are quite scarce. But one stamp of this issue stands out among the others. It is the 10-centavo without the surcharge. Only one example exists.

In 1919, Compania Colombiana de Navegacion Aerea, an aviation company, set up shop in Medellin, Colombia, to operate an internal mail service. The first test flight took place February 14, 1920. On February 22, the company began carrying mail on flights.

Since this was the first airmail service in Colombia, the Colombian Post Office had no official airmail stamps. The Colombian government gave Compania Colombiana permission to issue its own airmail stamps.

There was no time to have stamps printed, so the company obtained a set of advertising labels privately printed by the Curtis Motor & Aviation Company. The designs of these labels featured a woman and boy watching a plane; clouds and a small biplane; closeup view of a tilted plane; lighthouse; fuselage and tail of a biplane; condor on a cliff; plane at rest with the pilot in the foreground; and an ocean liner.

Compania Colombiana overprinted these labels "Compania Colombiana/de/Navegacion Aerea/Porte aereo: $0.10." One hundred of each design were surcharged.

Only one without the surcharge has been found used on cover. This cover was sent from Cartagena to Barranquilla. It was owned by Federico Larsen. H.R. Harmer, Inc., sold the cover at auction April 18, 1955. It later was acquired by John N. Myer.

This rarity currently is part of Alex Rendon's collection of Colombian airmail. It is one of the great treasures of airmail philately.

Pacific Perf Varieties

VALUE: $12,500

*Cook Islands rare 1892 1-penny
black imperf-between vertical pair.*

One of the great rarities of the Pacific islands is the Cook Islands 1892 1-penny black imperforate-between vertical pair. Cook Islands is located in the southeast Pacific Ocean about 2,000 miles northeast of New Zealand. Today, it is self-governing, with New Zealand retaining responsibility for defense and foreign affairs.

But in 1888, the islands were under the protection of Great Britain. Mail was handled through the British resident on the islands. In 1891, the British resident, Frederick Moss, appointed a postmaster to set up a more reliable postal system. The postmaster's first order of business was to obtain a supply of stamps for the islands.

The Government Printing Office in Wellington, New Zealand, was commissioned to print the stamps, and the New Zealand postal authorities agreed to recognize the validity of these issues.

According to B.W.H. Poole, a leading authority on the Cook Islands in the early part of this century, one original die, set from type and without value, was used for all four values of this first issue (1d, 1½d, 2½d and 10d). Poole said that four casts were taken from the original die, and the appropriate values were inserted.

From these secondary matrixes, six replicas were produced and arranged in two horizontal rows of three. The printer then reproduced these blocks of six 10 times and arranged them in two vertical rows to form the printing plates of 60 stamps. Poole thus concluded that there are six types of each value repeated 10 times in each sheet.

The stamp design consists of a Greek border with an ornamental pattern within. At the center are seven stars representing the inhabited islands of the archipelago, the largest star representing Raratonga, the capital. Above the stars is the inscription "POSTAGE/COOK ISLANDS"; below is "FEDERATION/ONE PENNY."

The stamps made their debut in 1892. Although they were normally perforated 12½, collectors soon discovered perforation varieties. The scarcest of these varieties are vertical imperf-between pairs. According to Poole, this was an omission of the perfs between the first and second rows of stamps on the sheet.

This variety is believed to have occurred only on one sheet, so it is probable that only six vertical imperf-between pairs exist. Scott catalog lists the variety at $12,500.

Fifty Too Many

VALUE: $8,000

This Czechoslovakia 50-haleru issue
was erroneously surcharged "50h."

Only 20 copies of a Czechoslovakia postage-due surcharge error have been discovered — all in used condition. From 1924 to 1927, the Czechoslovakian Post Office experienced a shortage of post-age-due stamps and a surplus of definitives. The logical solution: surcharge the definitives to meet the need for postage dues.

This was not the first time the Czechoslovakian Post Office had surcharged definitives for postage dues. The country's first issue, the Hradcany stamps, had been similarly surcharged in 1922. When the post office again found certain values of its postage dues in short supply in 1924, authorities ordered the surcharging not only of the Hradcany issue but also the first issue of postage-due stamps.

In 1927, surpluses of the Allegory of the Republic issue were surcharged to create postage dues. By this time, the surcharging had become a common practice. Perhaps too common. The printer became careless.

During the surcharging of the Allegory issues, he mistakenly surcharged the 50-haleru value with the inscription "DOPLATIT 50" (Postage Due 50). There was no reason to surcharge a 50h stamp with the same denomination that already was inscribed on the stamp. Actually, the 50h was not intended for surcharging at all. If it had been, the word "DOPLATIT" would have been sufficient.

Collectors are uncertain of the number of 50h stamps surcharged in error. Since only 20 copies have been discovered, it is likely only one sheet or a partial sheet was sent through the press. All recorded copies are postmarked "Praha 14." Scott catalog prices the error at $8,000.

Collectors are cautioned that fakes exist. The Czechoslovakian handbook, *Padelky Ceskoslovenskych Postovnich Znamek 1918-1939*, says forgers have used the 150h provisional postage due to create the 50h error. They select stamps on which the surcharge covers most of the original denomination and paint over the rest with a matching red color.

Number 1 is Number 2

VALUE: $23,966

This used block of four of Denmark's rarest stamp — the 1851 2 rigs-bank-skilling — was discovered in an old drawer in Denmark in 1984.

Denmark's No. 1 stamp — the 1851 2 rigsbank-skilling — actually is its second stamp, not its first. Although intended for release April 1, 1851, along with the 4rs, which really was Denmark's first stamp, the 2rs was delayed until May 1 of that year.

Denmark issued the 2rs to cover the rate for letters carried on its special Fodpost (Foot Post) in Copenhagen. This local delivery

51

service began in 1806. The Danish Post Office operated it for a few years. Then Henrik Riegels took it over as a private venture.

The Fodpost continued as a private venture until 1849, when the post office again assumed control. A fee of 2rs was charged for Fodpost letters delivered locally in Copenhagen.

The Danish Post Office commissioned Martinus William Ferslew to design and engrave Denmark's first stamps — the 4rs for ordinary inland letters and the 2rs for the Fodpost. Both stamps are square. The 2rs features the inscription "FRIMAERKE KGL. POST." in a circle with a crown at the top and posthorn at the bottom of the circle. In the center is the denomination, "2/RIGSBANK/SKILLING."

Ferslew was Denmark's finest engraver. He engraved several of its bank notes. Not only did he design and engrave Denmark's first stamp issue, he also printed the engraved burelage, the underprint of wavy lines used to prevent forgeries. Danish collectors question whether Ferslew also printed the stamp design of the 2rs, which was typographed. It is more likely that H.H. Thiele & Company printed the design.

A second printing of the 2rs made its debut in August 1852. This time Thiele typographed both the burelage and the design. Ferslew had died April 21 of that year.

The first printing is the scarcer of the two. According to *Denmark 2 Rigsbank-Skilling 1851-1852* by Sten Christensen, 1,018 sheets of 100 of the first printing and 3,775 sheets of 100 of the second printing were produced. Christensen also describes the printing plate produced by Ferslew.

The engraver made ten separate impressions of the original die in plaster. These were joined together in a block of ten — two vertical rows of five.

Ferslew prepared stereos from this block in type metal — ten for each plate with a few reserve blocks of ten. The ten blocks were soldered together to form each plate of 100 subjects.

Recognizable differences exist on the individual impressions of the original block of ten. Collectors refer to these as the "ten major types." Christensen describes these in detail.

Multiples of the 2rs are extremely scarce. Lars Amundsen and Alfred F. Lichtenstein, two great collectors, owned an unused block of four. This block was sold in the Dale-Lichtenstein sales by Harmers. Stanley Gibbons sold the block in 1977 by private treaty.

It is owned by Christian Andersen, a collector in Copenhagen.

In July 1984, 133 years after the stamp was issued, a used block of four of the 2rs was discovered in an old drawer in a town in western Denmark.

Globalia International Frimaerkeauktion, a Danish auction house, sold this block September 30, 1985, for 230,000 Danish kroner ($23,966), including a 15-percent buyer's premium.

Two other blocks are known to exist, but their whereabouts are unknown. Scott catalog lists singles of the first printing of the 2rs at $6,760 mint and $2,600 used. The second printing is priced at $4,000 mint and $1,300 used.

Only One Survivor

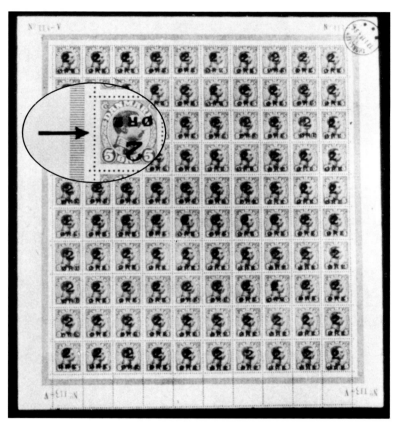

VALUE: $147,000

Stamp No. 21 in this sheet of the Faroese 1919 2-ore-on-5o provisional shows an inverted surcharge. Its existence was kept secret for 44 years.

For 44 years, stamp collectors were unaware of the existence of the Faroes' rarest stamp. The original owner kept his treasure a secret until his death. In 1962, Herbert Bernstein of Vineland, New Jersey, acquired a sheet of the Faroes 2-ore provisional of 1919 from the estate of the original owner. Not only is the sheet one of two existing complete sheets of this provisional, it also contains the only known copy with an inverted surcharge error.

Denmark increased its postal rates from 5 ore to 7o in January 1919. At this time, Europe was at war. Communications between Denmark and the Faroes, its possession in the North Atlantic, were poor, to say the least.

The Danish Post Office shipped a supply of 7o stamps to the Faroes, but to no one's surprise, it failed to reach the islands by the time the rate was placed into effect.

The Faroes was desperate for stamps to meet the new rate, so the Danish Post Office authorized Postmaster Godskesen Andersen in the Faroese capital of Thorshavn to surcharge sheets of the Danish 5o stamps with a 2o denomination. The surcharged stamps could be used in combination with 5o stamps to meet the new 7o postal rate.

The surcharging was done by hand. Apparently, the printer accidently turned the handstamping device upside down one time, thus accounting for one stamp with the surcharge inverted. Andersen reported that 155 sheets of 100 stamps were surcharged. Today, only two complete sheets of the provisional issue exist. One contains the error. The other, which belongs to the Danish Postal Museum, shows no error.

No sheets were sold intact. Only clerks at the post office were allowed to apply the surcharged stamps to mail. Stamp collectors were unable to buy stamps for their collection. All the surcharged issues which were sold were used on mail, accounting for the scarcity of unused stamps and complete sheets. These surcharged issues were on sale for only 10 days before the new 7o stamps arrived.

In 1976, the sheet containing the error was sold in Denmark by Danam Stamp Company. Robert Bechsgaard, a Danish dealer, paid $70,000. In less than 10 years, Bechsgaard more than doubled his investment. In July 1985, he sold the sheet for a record $147,000 to a collector in the United States. This is believed to be the highest price paid for a Danish or Faroese issue.

Times Express Locals

VALUE: $18,400

The Fiji Times Express 3-penny and 6d are featured on a cover addressed to Victoria, via Sydney, where a New South Wales 3d was added.

G.L. Griffiths had an ulterior motive when he started the Fiji Times Express mail service on Fiji in 1870. Not only was he concerned with moving the mails of the islanders, he also needed a more efficient mail service for his newspaper, the *Fiji Times*.

The enterprising Griffiths wanted to publish a biweekly newspaper, but the mail system in Fiji was too primitive to make such a venture possible. So Griffiths established his own mail service. He also issued stamps for this service — crude typeset issues with the denomination in the center and "FIJI TIMES EXPRESS" around the outer edge.

The first issue of these stamps was printed on pink quadrille paper. It consisted of four values — 1 penny, 3d, 6d and 1/-.

Griffiths announced the establishment of his mail service in the October 8, 1870, issue of the *Fiji Times*. The advertisement read:

"Remember, remember the First of November

"The day you'll have reason to bless,

"For then we commence a thing quite immense
"To be called the Fiji Times Express."

The Fiji Times Express stamps could be considered locals because they were intended for use only on the islands. Letters being mailed to New Zealand, for example, had to have New Zealand stamps affixed.

In 1871, a second set of stamps made its debut, this time on laid batonne paper. The second printing featured the same design and values as the first. A 9d denomination was added.

In *Fiji Islands*, C.J. Phillips explained that the 9d was made by lifting the figure "3" from the 3d stamp on three positions on the plate and substituting the figure "9."

The first set is scarcer than the second, although collectors disagree on the printing totals. Phillips quotes Griffiths as being "confident that not less than 100,000 stamps were put into circulation." J.G. Rodger and R.F. Duberal, in *Fiji: The Stamps and Postal History 1870-75*, dispute this. They say no more than 2,400 of each of the commonest stamps and only about 12,000 altogether were released. John Gartner, in his pamphlet *On the Stamps of Fiji*, estimates that 600 each on quadrille paper and 2,400 each on batonne paper were issued.

Collectors do agree that these stamps are scarce, particularly when found on piece or on cover. Scott catalog prices for these issues range from $1,500 to $4,000. David Feldman sold an 1871 cover, bearing the 3d and 6d Fiji Times Express stamps, at his AMERIPEX auction May 30, 1986. The cover realized $18,400, including a 15-percent buyer's premium. It is addressed to Victoria, via Sydney, where a New South Wales 3d stamp was added.

Official imitations of the Fiji Times Express stamps exist on pink laid paper, pin perforated, and on pink wove paper. These are not reprints since they were not produced from the original plate. The first of these was created to satisfy requests of overseas collectors who could not obtain copies of the genuine stamps.

In 1871, King Cakobau set up a constitutional government in Fiji and established an official postal system. Griffiths was notified to cease operations. The Fiji Times Express thus came to an end in 1872. In less than two years, Griffiths greatly improved Fiji's mail service and created stamps whose scarcity and history have long intrigued collectors.

Reduced to Ashes

VALUE: $32,500

The ex-Cox example of the Fiji error is the only one in private hands.

A tragic fire contributed to the scarcity of the already-rare Fiji 1878-91 2-penny ultramarine error of color. Now only one example of this stamp remains in private hands. Another is in the Queen's Royal Collection in England. It is highly unlikely this example ever will be offered for sale.

In 1878, a new series of stamps was introduced by Fiji, featuring the "V.R." (Victoria Regina) monogram surmounted by a crown. The 1-penny and 2d values of this series were printed in ultramarine and green, respectively.

On March 28, 1881, John B. Thurston of the Colonial Secretary's Office ordered 50,000 2d green and 30,000 6d bright rose stamps from the Government Printing Office in Sydney, Australia. The stamps were printed and shipped by *SS Gunga* on April 11. When the order arrived, however, it was discovered that the 2d was printed in ultramarine instead of green.

According to Charles J. Phillips' study of the Fiji Islands, Thurston acknowledged receipt of the stamps on May 3, 1881, but pointed out the 2d color error. He requested a new shipment of this denomination in the proper green color.

In the January-February 1987 *London Philatelist*, John B. Marriott, keeper of the Royal Collection, discusses the Fiji error of color. Marriott says that on December 19, 1889, the receiver general, in response to an inquiry from the colonial secretary, sent four of the color errors and reported that "about 50,000 were on hand."

On December 24, 1889, the colonial secretary, wrote to the Crown Agents, enclosed "a few specimens" of the error and sug-

The Ferrari copy of the Fiji error of color was destroyed by fire in 1983.

gested that perhaps Messrs. Thompson might care to purchase some of the stamps. The British Library says it has an unused copy of the error in the Crown Agents Philatelic and Security Printing Archive. According to Library officials, the copy is affixed to page 53 of the volume marked "Crown Agents for the Colonies/Stamp Album/Vol. 1/Adhesive Stamps."

According to Marriott, T.H. Thompson & Company of Bishop Auckland previously had bought a large quantity of so-called obsolete Fiji stamps. Marriott says prudence prevailed, however, and

Governor Thurston decided the errors should be "destroyed forthwith." Fiji archival material includes a July 24, 1890, entry stating, "We have this day destroyed by fire 49,940 Postage Stamps (twopenny stamps colored blue in error) — R. Scott, D.J. Chisholm."

It is not known what happened to the four 2d stamps sent by the receiver general. Marriott says it also is unknown whether there was any discrepancy between the figures of "about 50,000" and "49,940 Postage Stamps" destroyed.

The first mention of this error in the philatelic press appeared in

This Fiji color error was added to the Royal Collection by King George V.

the December 1892 *London Philatelist.* This issue states, on the authority of Hilckes, Kirkpatrick and Company, that only one example of the error was saved. They sold it to a well-known collector, the Parisian, Count Ferrari.

The company also produced official documents saying the entire printing had been destroyed, except for this one stamp. Two other copies eventually came to light.

In a paper read before the Royal Philatelic Society of London on November 4, 1926, E.D. Bacon referred to the example in the Royal

Collection. He said, "It is believed that these two specimens (Ferrari and Royal Collection) are the only ones now in existence."

Marriott says little is known about the example in the Royal Collection. He says it was acquired before November 4, 1926, when Bacon referred to it, and after March 6, 1913, since it was not mentioned in Tilleard's paper on that date to the RPSL.

The Ferrari example received little prominence when the count's collection was auctioned. The stamp was sold as part of a lot of 164 stamps in the seventh Ferrari sale on June 14, 1923. It was mentioned, but not illustrated. It had pulled or torn perforations at the top right side. Of the three copies recorded, this was of the poorest condition. Arthur Hind purchased this example. In the fifth Hind sale conducted by H.R. Harmer of London, the stamp was listed and illustrated as lot 36. It sold for £40. The stamp then became part of the Purves collection.

In *The Postage Stamps of Fiji 1878-1902*, J.R.W. Purves identified the stamp as No. 24 of the lower pane. He said the ultramarine color of the stamp was different from any shade found in the 1d ultramarine. In the April 27, 1953, Colonel Hans Lagerloef sale by H.R. Harmer of New York, this example was listed and illustrated as lot 247. Marriott says Sir Lacon Threlford owned the stamp as early as 1958 when he showed it in his display at the Royal Philatelic Society. On June 16, 1975, H.R. Harmer of London auctioned the stamp as lot 130 in its Threlford sale.

John Gartner of Australia purchased the rarity. He was to be the last owner of this rarity.

On February 16, 1983, Ash Wednesday, Gartner and his wife sat in their home in Mount Macedon, Victoria, Australia, listening to reports of bushfires 20 miles away. They went to bed with no signs of imminent danger. Suddenly, the wind shifted. Gale forces began shooting balls of fire from debris at Mount Macedon and at the Gartner home.

The whole town was aflame. Gartner and his wife grabbed two woolen blankets, put them over their heads, ran out of the house and jumped into their swimming pool. From the pool, they watched as their home, valued at $650,000, burned to the ground, taking with it all their possessions, including Gartner's fabulous collections of Fiji, Sarawak and Hong Kong, and his 25,000-volume library. The Fiji error of color went up in smoke, reducing the number in private hands to one.

The third example of the error was sold in the A.W. Cox auction by H.R. Harmer of London September 25-26, 1933, as lot 379. This stamp, the finest of the three, was sold by private treaty by Harmers of New York during the AMERIPEX '86 international stamp show in Chicago in 1986. This now is the only copy of the rarity in private hands. Scott catalog lists the error of color at $32,500.

Murphy Strikes Again

VALUE: $6,250

The 5-penni error of color was printed in buff instead of red-brown.

VALUE: Indeterminable

Caspary owned this 10p red-brown error in a tete-beche pair with the 5p.

Murphy's law ("what can go wrong will go wrong") can be blamed for the printing errors which occurred on the 5-penni and 10p stamps of Finland's 1866-74 series.

In November 1865, Finland reformed its monetary system from Russian currency (rubles and kopecks) to a new Finnish currency (markkaa and penni). The Finnish Post Office ordered a new series of stamps reflecting this change.

The stamps were similar in design to the previous series, featuring the Finnish coat of arms. The printer continued to use serpentine rouletting to separate the stamps. But this process was slow because only one sheet could be rouletted at a time. So, more than one rouletting instrument was used.

Since each differed from the other, four different types of indentations exist. Type I is 1 millimeter to 1¼mm in depth; type II, 1½mm to 1¾mm; type III, 2mm to 2¼mm; and type IV, with shovel-shaped teeth, 1¼mm to 1½mm.

In 1868, a British collector discovered copies of the 5p and 10p stamps of the 1866-74 series in the wrong colors. The 5p was printed in the buff color of the 10p and the 10p in the red brown of the 5p. The errors exist only with the type III rouletting.

The collector contacted the Finnish Post Office for an explanation. The post office immediately began a search for additional copies of the errors and ordered their withdrawal from sale at post

VALUE: $10,000

A tete-beche pair of Finland's 5-penni red-brown stamp is shown used with a normal pair of the stamp. The strip was in the Faberge collection.

offices throughout Finland. Two thousand errors existed; 1,435 5p and 1,000 2p were returned. The post office burned these copies.

Upon investigating, the printer found that when the cliches were taken apart for cleaning, which was done after each printing, some were inserted into the wrong frames. The 5p cliche was inserted in the frame of the 10p and the 10p in the frame of the 5p.

When the color errors were discovered, the printer removed the erroneous cliches and inserted the correct values. The printer made one more mistake. He replaced a 10p cliche with the correct 5p, but inserted it upside down, creating the 5p tete-beche variety.

Only a few such pairs exist. Scott catalog lists this variety at $10,000. Alfred Caspary, who owned a remarkable collection of 19th-century worldwide stamps, owned a piece showing the 10p red-brown color error in a horizontal tete-beche pair with the 5p. The piece formerly was in the Lindberg collection. Scott catalog prices the 5p buff color error at $6,250; the 10p red-brown error at $6,000 mint and $3,500 used.

A Ceres Mistake

VALUE: $4,250

France's scarce 15-centime bister cliche error of the 1872-75 series is shown in this se-tenant pair with the normal 10c bister-on-rose stamp.

France offers many rarities among its classic issues. One, while not as scarce as some, is nonetheless a striking error. Imagine finding a se-tenant pair of stamps with the same design, in the same color, but with two different values. This is exactly what Arthur Maury was searching for in 1876 when he scoured the post offices of Paris.

Maury, now famous for the Maury French specialized catalog, visited every post office in Paris in search of a mysterious 15-centime error. He had discovered a 15-centime stamp of France printed in the bister-on-rose color of the 1875 10c.

Both values were part of the 1872-75 issue featuring the portrait of Ceres. However, the 15c was printed in bister, not bister on rose. Maury searched the post offices for copies of this error. He finally found 200 at the Place de la Bourse. He bought all 200.

When the French Post Office learned of Maury's discovery, it recalled the 15c from sale. As a result of the error, the post office ordered the printing of a new series featuring the Sage design of "Peace and Commerce." The Sage type series continued in use until the turn of the century.

Who was responsible for the 15c bister-on-rose error? The famous Anatole Hulot, the printer who also created France's earlier tete-beche varieties. Hulot, or more likely one of his employees, mistakenly inserted a cliche of the 15c value in a sheet of 150 of the 10c Ceres stamp.

Although this error does not compare in price to most of the earlier tete-beche varieties — which bring five- and six-figure prices when sold — the error is scarce nonetheless. Scott catalog lists singles at $3,250 mint and $3,500 used.

Even scarcer is the error se-tenant with the 10c. These pairs catalog at $4,250 mint and $4,500 used. A most remarkable item is a French formula card franked with a vertical pair of the 10c and the 15c error. Forgeries of this error are common.

Dark Red Saxon

VALUE: $275,000

The only known used block of four of the 1850 Saxony 3-pfennig cherry red variety is canceled with a clear double-circle "CHEMNITZ 10 AUG 50."

Saxony's first issue — the 3-pfennig red of 1850 — is one of the most sought after stamps of the German States. Although not as famous as Saxony's ½-neu-groschen pale blue error, the stamp nevertheless is a great rarity, particularly the dark red variety.

When Saxony joined the German-Austrian Postal Union in 1850, the need for stamps to prepay postage became apparent. The postal officials of Saxony called upon their Bavarian neighbors for guidance in producing their first stamps.

The simple design copied Bavaria's 1849 issue. It features an open numeral "3" with a mazework pattern on a background composed of wavy lines. The frame reads "SACHSEN" at the top, "DREI" at left and "PFENNIGE" at right, and "FRANCO" at the bottom. An ornamental design appears in each corner.

The imperforate stamp was typographed on unwatermarked paper by J.B. Hirschfield in Leipzig. Printer's rules were placed between the casts. As can be seen in the illustrated block of four, the horizontal lines are continuous. The vertical lines were cut so they are as high as the design but do not touch the horizontal line.

A half million stamps were printed. Of this half million, 463,058 were sold by the post office. When the post office withdrew the issue from sale, it burned 36,922.

This raises the question: Why is this issue so scarce today? The 3pf covered the rate on journals and printed matter. Although it was first sold June 29, 1850, the new stamp was not valid for postage until July 1.

Beginning July 1, however, the use of this stamp to prepay postage on printed matter was mandatory. If the stamp was not affixed, the post office charged the full letter rate.

These stamps confused Saxons. They were uncertain where the stamps should be placed. Instead of affixing them to the upper right-hand corner, the Saxons usually stuck the stamps partly on the wrapper and partly on the newspaper to prevent the paper from slipping out. Recipients ripped open the wrapper, destroying the stamp in the process.

For this reason, few 3pf stamps exist today. This issue is one of the rarest of the German States. Extremely scarce are the color varieties.

Noted collector John F. Seybold owned two covers, each bearing a pair of what Scott catalog refers to as the dark red variety. Seybold also owned three singles and a strip of three. United States pharmaceutical magnate Josiah K. Lilly owned a right sheet margin block of four. Robert A. Siegel sold this block in 1967 for $25,000.

John R. Boker Jr. owned a used block of four of what the Michel German specialized catalog refers to as the cherry red variety. This block, the only used block of four known to exist of this variety, realized 500,000 Deutsche marks (about U.S. $275,000) when it was sold by Heinrich Kohler during the March 14, 1987, auction in

Wiesbaden, West Germany.

In the April 1980 *German Postal Specialist*, the journal of the Germany Philatelic Society, Dr. Werner M. Bohne illustrated one of the few perfect copies of the normal 3pf red on complete wrapper. The bottom portion of the stamp is affixed to the wrapper, but the upper portion still shows original gum. Dr. Bohne says it appears the sender only "licked" the lower part of the stamp. In the article, he warns that most 3pf covers have been repaired and should be expertized.

Scott catalog lists the 3pf red at $6,500 mint and $6,250 used. It prices the dark red variety at $12,000 mint or used. A repaired single sold for $770, including a 10-percent buyer's premium, at the Robert A. Siegel November 21-25, 1985, auction. A vertical pair on cover realized $24,200, including a 10-percent buyer's premium, at David Feldman's AMERIPEX auction May 30, 1986.

Boxer Rebellion Provisional

VALUE: $32,500

Mint copy of the rare Tientsin 50-pfennig handoverprint of 1900.

VALUE: $18,500

A used copy of the Offices in China provisional with a Tientsin postmark.

Collectors question the legitimacy of the Tientsin provisionals, but that does not stop them from paying high prices for them when they come up for sale.

In 1899, a secret Chinese society, I Ho Ch'uan, led a revolt, with the support of Dowager Empress Tz'u Hsi, against the widening interests of foreign powers in China. This revolt is known as the Boxer Rebellion. Foreign powers sent troops into China to quash the rebellion. Some foreign powers issued stamps for their post offices in China. Germany was among these.

At first, Germany used its regular issues at its post offices in China. The postal headquarters in Berlin later began overprinting these stamps with "China" running diagonally across the stamp.

In 1900, a supply of Germany's Reichpost issue featuring Germania was sent to the post office in the city of Tientsin. The stamps bore no overprint, so the postmaster took it upon himself to handstamp "China" on these issues. He made no effort to contact postal headquarters in Berlin to obtain permission to overprint the issue. There was no time.

When correspondence bearing these stamps began filtering through the home office in Germany, postal officials faced a dilemma. Should they accept the overprints, although they were unauthorized, or should they reject them? It would have been more of a problem to reject the stamps. The overprints were accepted.

The Tientsin postmaster overprinted seven values of the Reichpost set. Although each overprinted stamp catalogs at more than $300, the 50 pfennigs is the scarcest. Scott catalog lists it at $32,500 mint and $18,500 used. The 30pf is listed at $8,000 both mint and used, and the 80pf catalogs at $5,000 mint, $4,500 used.

Because the stamps were overprinted by hand, varieties abound. The overprint is known inverted, doubled and running from top left to bottom right instead of the normal bottom left to top right.

Unfortunately, this issue also attracts forgers. Faked handstamps are common. Forgeries of the 50pf recently turned up on the market in Germany, creating havoc among stamp dealers, collectors, expertizers and auction houses.

'Yellow Dog' Varieties

VALUE: $16,400 plus

Both stamps in this pair of Germany's Gelber Hund issue feature the inverted overprint and surcharge. The right stamp shows the "Huna" variety.

"Gelber Hund," German for "Yellow Dog," may seem an unusual overprint on a stamp. But the *Gelber Hund* was an airplane, and the semiofficial stamps bearing this overprint were used on mail carried by the plane. In 1912, the grand duke and duchess of Hessen, Germany, granted their patronage to the first German airmail flight along the Rhine.

The Center for Mother and Infant Care, of which the duke and duchess were patrons, sponsored a Postcard Week in conjunction with the flight to raise funds for the center. The event originally was scheduled for June 10-17, 1912, but was extended to June 23 by the organizers.

Special postcards and stamps were produced for this charity event. Although the stamps were sanctioned by the German postal authorities, the cards bearing them had to be franked with regular postage in addition to the airmail issue.

The German Government Printing Works in Berlin produced 10-pfennig red brown, 20pf red brown and 30pf green stamps. Each featured a letter-carrying bird in the center above the sun and a cloud. The inscription in the circle surrounding the design read: "ERSTE DEUTSCHE LUFTPOST AM RHEIN" (First German Airpost on the Rhine). The stamps were sold in the post offices of the five airport cities along the Rhine — Darmstadt, Frankfurt, Mainz, Offenbach and Worms.

Two types of aircraft were used to carry mail on this occasion — the zeppelin *Schwaben* and the Euler biplane *Gelber Hund*, piloted by Lieutenant Hidessen. Collectors can obtain zeppelin and airplane flown cards for this event.

In *Airmails 1870-1970*, author James Mackay tells an interesting tale about the naming of the biplane. He says, "The story of how this aircraft got its name is an amusing one. One stormy day the biplane, whose wings were painted yellow, refused to rise. The quick-tempered Hidessen exclaimed angrily, 'Hatte ich dich nur oben, du gelber Hund!' (If only I had you up, you yellow dog). The constructor, Euler, overheard this remark and promptly dubbed the recalcitrant aeroplane the Gelber Hund."

A higher fee was required for mail transported by the airplane than that carried on the zeppelin. To meet this higher rate, the 10pf stamps were overprinted "Gelber Hund" diagonally and surcharged with a new "1 M" (1 mark) value.

As with most overprinted stamps, errors occurred. "Huna," instead of "Hund," is found on some stamps. This variety occurred when the "d" in "Hund" was damaged, resulting in what appears to be an "a." Inverted overprints and surcharges also have been discovered. They command high prices when sold.

However, the most extraordinary of these errors is a pair, believed to be unique, featuring both the "Huna" variety and the inverted overprint and surcharge. The overprint and surcharge are inverted on both stamps in the pair. The right stamp features the "Huna" variety, while the left shows the normal "Hund." Collectors are cautioned that forgeries of these stamps exist. Forgers create the "Huna" variety by erasing part of the "d."

Since the genuine Yellow Dog stamps are semiofficial in nature, they are not listed in Scott catalog. The Michel *Deutschland-Spezial* (German specialized catalog) lists mint stamps with the inverted surcharge and overprint at 35,000m (about $16,400). Imagine what the pair showing both varieties would sell for today.

In *Pioneer Airpost Flights of the World 1830-1935*, author Dr. Max Kronstein says 460,700 postcards were flown from June 10 to June 23. He says this makes it the largest semiofficial airpost service in Europe before World War I. The 10pf and 20pf stamps later were overprinted "E.EL.P.," an abbreviation for "Ex Est Luftpost" (Airpost Comes to an End). These overprinted issues exist on cards flown the last day of the event, June 23.

Thank the Thieves

VALUE: $7,500

*Thieves created a rarity when they
stole several sheets of this 20/- stamp.*

Thieves are responsible for the scarcity of a stamp of Gold
Coast, a former British crown colony (now Ghana) in west Africa. In
1889, Gold Coast issued three high-denominated stamps — 5 shillings, 10/-, and 20/- — portraying Queen Victoria.

These issues were intended mostly for fiscal purposes. However,
they carried the inscription "POSTAGE/REVENUE," so they could
be used on letters as well.

Janitors at the Gold Coast Post Office realized the potential value
of these high-denominated stamps. They banded together and de-
vised a scheme to steal the stamps. One night, when all the postal
workers had gone, the janitors broke into the vaults and ran off with
24 sheets of the 20/- green and red.

Two months passed before postal officials suspected anything.
While taking inventory of the stock, an official noticed the sheets
were missing.

To discourage speculation, the post office ordered the immediate withdrawal of the 20/- from sale. In 1894, a new 20/- was issued, this time in different colors (violet and black), to replace the withdrawn stamps.

The thieves weren't as clever as it may seem. The police eventually traced the missing stamps back to the janitors. They were arrested and convicted.

In his book, *Rare Stamps*, L.N. Williams gives an account of this story. He says 1,000 of the stolen stamps were recovered. The post office destroyed these stamps, along with the sheets which were withdrawn from sale.

Only a few unused examples of the 20/- green and red exist. No used examples have been discovered. Scott catalog prices this stamp at $7,500. The thieves succeeded in one respect. They created a philatelic rarity.

B-Blank Error

VALUE: $6,500
"B-blank" error with the letter "A" missing in the lower right-hand corner.

Two philatelic writers drew collectors' attention to what was to become a rare British philatelic error. In the 1890s, while researching material for their book, *History of the Adhesive Stamps of the British Isles*, Hastings E. Wright and A.B. Creeke Jr. examined the registration sheets of Britain's 1841 1-penny red brown. These sheets were in the British Post Office archives in Somerset House, the headquarters of the British Inland Revenue.

The authors discovered that the check letter "A" was omitted from the lower right-hand corner of the first stamp in the second row on a sheet from plate 77. The left-hand corner bore the letter "B." Check letters were used on early British stamps to prevent forgeries. They indicated the position of each stamp in the sheet.

For example, the first stamp was lettered "A-A," the second "A-B," the first stamp in the second row "B-A," etc. The letters were individually hand-punched into the plate. Each stamp on the sheet had a different combination of letters. A forger would find it extremely difficult to come up with the correct combination. This also discouraged the cutting up and joining of parts of used stamps to deceive the Post Office.

Wright and Creeke learned that Edwin Hill, the inspector of stamps at Somerset House, had discovered the missing letter error after a few sheets had been printed. Hill informed the printer, Perkins, Bacon & Company. He asked the printer to insert the letter "A" in the blank space. The corrected plate was registered as plate 77b.

Wright and Creek disclosed the error — known as the "B-blank" error — in their book. However, it was not until 1905 that a stamp showing the error was discovered. This stamp was exhibited in London that year.

Several copies have since been found. Two exist on cover. The rarity is listed in Scott at $6,500.

Check the Plate Number

VALUE: $82,500

Great Britain's rare 1864 Penny Red stamp, with plate number 77, is used on piece with a 4d stamp.

The plate numbers on early British stamps often distinguish between a common stamp and a great rarity. A prime example of this is the 1864 Penny Red. Most of the stamps in this issue catalog from a few cents to hundreds of dollars. But Scott lists a Penny Red from plate 77 at $60,000 unused and $40,000 used. The plate number makes a significant difference in price.

The British Post Office issued the world's first adhesive postage stamp in 1840 and from the beginning realized that the public would try to find ways to reuse these stamps. Several security measures were attempted, including fugitive colors and various cancellations.

In 1858, postal authorities decided to produce stamps with check letters in all four corners to further discourage reuse. Unscrupulous persons had been known to piece together two used stamp halves which had not been spoiled by cancellations. The letters in the four corners would make it impossible to piece together stamps and arrive at the appropriate combinations of letters.

At the same time it adopted the letters in the four corners, the

British Post Office decided to place the plate number at the side of each stamp in the network design. The first stamps featuring the plate number and the check letters in all four corners were introduced in 1858.

Although plates for the 1d were produced at this time, the Penny Red stamps with the four check letters were not issued until 1864. Plates 69-228 were assigned for the 1d stamp by the printer, Perkins, Bacon. Plates 69, 70, 75, 77, 126 and 128 were rejected. Plates 226, 227 and 228 were laid down, but they were never used because the Perkins, Bacon contract expired.

Although plate 77 was rejected because of irregular spacing of the stamp subjects, a few sheets were printed and found their way into circulation, accounting for the great rarities which exist today.

In *A History of British Postage Stamps*, T. Todd says Sir Edward Bacon suggested that these stamps were trials printed before plate 77 was rejected. Sir Edward wrote, "These trial stamps may then have been mixed in with the ordinary stock and put into circulation in the usual way, or they may have been put on one side, and perhaps after an interval, used by some official or other individual who came across them."

Nine stamps from plate 77 have been recorded — four unused and five used. Of the unused copies, one lettered BA-AB is in the Royal Collection at Buckingham Palace, and another lettered AB-BA is in the Tapling Collection at the British Library in London.

In *Rare Stamps*, L.N. and M. Williams say a third example lettered CA-AC was discovered in 1919. This stamp realized £1,700 at the sale of the J. de R. Phillp collection and later was acquired by Major C.E. Raphael. According to the Williams brothers, Major Raphael's collection of Great Britain was stolen in February 1965. The present whereabouts of this copy of the 1d stamp are unknown. Another unused 1d from plate 77 has been recorded, but its lettering is not known.

Of the five used copies, one owned by H.J. Crocker was destroyed during the San Francisco earthquake in 1906, along with several other items from Crocker's collection. A 1d plate 77 used on piece with a 4d was auctioned by Christie's/Robson Lowe March 11, 1987, as part of the Isleham collection. It realized $82,500, including a 10-percent buyer's premium.

Queen Victoria's Abnormal

VALUE: $20,000

*Only two unused examples exist of
the 10 pence plate 2 abnormal.*

Among the rarest of the British abnormals is the 1867-80 10 pence from plate 2. This plate was prepared by the London printer Thomas De La Rue but never sent to press. Fewer than 50 copies of this 10d exist. Only two unused examples have been recorded.

The abnormals are British surface-printed stamps produced during the reign of Queen Victoria. For each plate, it was customary for six proof sheets to be printed. One of these sheets (known as an imprimatur) went into the archives of the British Post Office. The others sometimes were perforated and issued, although they frequently differed from the regularly issued stamps in color, paper, watermark or perforation.

Great Britain released the 10d Queen Victoria stamp in 1867 to meet the postal rate to India, Mauritius and Australia.

According to John Easton's *The De La Rue History of British and Foreign Postage Stamps*, plate 1 was registered March 22, 1867. However, De La Rue experienced problems in the positioning of the electrotypes on plate 1, causing perforating difficulties. A new plate was ordered.

Plate 2 was produced and registered August 30, 1867. But by this time, the British Post Office realized there was little demand for the 10d value. Except for the proof sheets, the plate for this value was never sent to press.

The 10d plate 2 is printed in pale red brown. The plate number appears in circles above the lower letter squares. The most remarkable examples of this 10d abnormal are the two unused copies and a used pair. L.N. Williams, the well-known philatelic author who has studied the British abnormals extensively, says the pair is the only known example of a used abnormal in multiple. The lower letter squares of the pair bear the letters P-C and P-D.

One of the unused copies is in the Royal Collection at Buckingham Palace. This stamp has been repaired. In 1978, David Feldman of Switzerland offered an unused 10d plate 2 in a private treaty sale. This copy is lettered T-A.

Most used copies of this abnormal are found on letters sent by Messrs. Crosse & Blackwell to their agents in India. Scott catalog lists the 10d plate 2 at $20,000 unused and $4,000 used.

No Crown for the Queen

VALUE: Indeterminable

*Only one copy exists of this British 1-penny stamp of
1880 printed in error on Orb watermarked paper.*

The discovery of a British error was revealed in 1968. Little was known of the stamp at that time, and today, nearly 20 years later, it still remains a mystery. This rarity is the Great Britain 1-penny red-brown, also known as venetian red, printed in error on Orb water-marked paper. This issue normally was printed on Crown water-marked paper.

The 1880 1d surface-printed issue came into being as a result of the British Post Office's efforts to discourage reusing postage stamps. Stamp washing has troubled postal authorities since the first stamp was issued in 1840. With the release of the Penny Black, the British Post Office concerned itself with finding ways to prevent the reuse of these stamps. This battle continues today with postal authorities forever searching for ways to prevent the removal of cancellations.

During the 19th century, the British Post Office experimented with various printing processes, hoping one would deter the reuse of stamps. De La Rue and Company, the printer of many British stamps, used fugitive inks to prevent stamp washing.

In 1878, De La Rue surface-printed all British issues with face values of 2d and above. Perkins, Bacon and Petch line engraved the low values — ½d, 1d and 1½d. The surface-printed stamps were produced in fugitive inks. The line-engraved issues were not.

In 1878, The British Board of Inland Revenue informed Perkins, Bacon and Petch that the ½d, 1d and 1½d stamps also were to be surface-printed to prevent the washing of these values. The printer experimented with fugitive inks but was unsuccessful in its renewal bid for the printing contract. The contract for the three low values, as well as the higher values, went to De La Rue.

The first stamp to be printed under this new agreement was the 1d red-brown. This denomination, like the others in this series, was printed on watermarked paper featuring the imperial crown. However, the stamp discovered in 1968 is on paper with the watermark showing an orb.

Stanley Gibbons' *British Commonwealth Catalogue, Part 1* does not list this error. Gibbons does mention it in Volume I of the *Great Britain Specialised Catalogue* covering the Queen Victoria period. The editors of the catalog say: "A copy of this stamp was reported in 1968 to exist with watermark Orb (Fiscal Orb), but until we have evidence of further examples or more information is forthcoming we will defer listing at the present time." Scott catalog does list the stamp as 79b but does not include a price.

This error was sold by Robson Lowe in his December 13, 1979, auction. At that time, the auction catalog touted the stamp as "Great Britain's Rarest Stamp." It realized £4,750. The stamp is used on a small piece postmarked "LONDON EC 6 MR 1782." In 20 years, no additional copies have been discovered, and no new information has come to light. It may be "Great Britain's rarest stamp," but it also is one of its greatest mysteries.

Parcels From the Government

VALUE: $10,000

The discovery of this copy of the inverted error on an original piece established the credibility of the error.

One of Great Britain's notable philatelic rarities suffered a rocky history with collectors. In 1883, the British Post Office began overprinting current Queen Victoria stamps with the inscription "GOVT/PARCELS" for use by all government departments. Similar stamps were overprinted through 1902.

Soon after the release of the 1-shilling Government Parcel Official, collectors discovered copies of this stamp with inverted overprints. These discoveries generated much excitement in the philatelic world. Stamp catalogs began listing the error. Scott catalog listed it, but without a price.

A few years later, collectors began to study the invert. Experts declared the copies forgeries. Catalog editors removed the listing of the error.

But in the 1940s, British stamp dealer Harry Nissen redeemed the inverted overprint to its status as a genuine error when he discovered a copy affixed to a piece of an original parcel post label. The piece is from the Mount Pleasant Parcel Office in London. It is inscribed "ON HER MAJESTY'S SERVICE." The stamp is tied by a "LONDON" cancel. Catalogs once again listed the error. The current Scott catalog prices it at $10,000 used.

Stanley Gibbons in London auctioned the copy on piece in 1978 for £4,000 (about $7,200). It is the only example known on piece. Ten copies of the inverted overprint have been certified as genuine. Forgeries still exist of the 1/- inverted overprint.

A similar error also occurs on the 1-penny Government Parcels Official of 1897. This is listed in Scott catalog at $1,300 mint and $700 used.

Strange Salmon Shade

VALUE: $2,000
*A copy of the scarce salmon shade
of the Greek 1862-67 10-lepta issue.*

A strange color shade and a rarity lurks among the 1862-67 10-lepta Large Hermes Head stamps of Greece. This denomination, normally found in shades of yellow-orange, also exists in a seldom seen salmon shade. Only three 10-lepta stamps in this shade have been discovered. But collectors have been unable to explain how the shade occurred.

The Large Hermes Heads are the first issue of Greece. The earliest stamps in this series were printed in Paris. However, later in 1861, the printing of Greek stamps was moved to Athens, hence the designations Paris and Athens printings. The rare 10-lepta salmon shade is part of the second Athens printing (1862-67).

Robson Lowe, the eminent stamp dealer and collector in England, says the 10-lepta salmon was issued circa 1863. The delicately printed yellow-orange control numerals and greenish paper conform to those used that year.

The distinctive salmon shade, however, differs from any previous or subsequent printings of the Large Hermes Heads.

An unused example of the 10-lepta salmon was auctioned by Robson Lowe in Zurich May 31, 1983. The stamp realized 4,300 Swiss francs (about $2,000).

Lowe says correspondence between Edwin Luder and collector Julio Philippi in 1949 mentions two other examples of this 10-lepta shade variety, one of which was used. Lowe also recalls that P.L. Pemberton showed him an example, referring to it as one of the rarest Greek classics.

Since at least three copies of this shade exist, it can be assumed the stamps are true varieties, not color changelings.

Deal for the Birds

VALUE: $4,000
*Guatemala's scarce 5-centavo Small
Quetzal of 1881 with inverted center.*

Guatemala's most famous errors — the upside down Small Quetzals — were produced in the United States by the American Bank Note Company. In 1881, the government of Guatemala ordered a new set of stamps to be printed by ABNC, which also had printed Guatemala's previous issue. The new set consisted of five values — 1 centavo, 2c, 5c, 10c and 20c.

ABNC printed the center of each of the beautifully engraved stamps in green. The center features the quetzal, Guatemala's national bird. The borders of the stamps, which show the value and the inscription "UNION POSTAL UNIVERSAL-GUATEMALA," were printed in black, brown, red, lilac and yellow, respectively.

ABNC used the same plates for the centers of the 1881 as were used for the 1879 stamps. New plates were produced for the frames. The stamps refer to the Universal Postal Union because Guatemala had recently joined the UPU.

This Small Quetzal issue went on sale November 7, 1881. In a most unusual move, the stamps were demonetized July 1, 1886, as part of a deal struck between the Guatemalan government and a British engineer, Charles Parker, who was employed by the government. Stamp collectors believe Parker was acting on behalf of New York stamp dealer H.L. Calman.

Parker suggested that Guatemala issue a set of high value provisional stamps which he would provide at his own expense. The 1881 Small Quetzals were to be demonetized and replaced by provisional issues until the new stamps could be printed.

As soon as Parker delivered the new stamps, he would receive, as compensation, all the 1881 Small Quetzals and the provisionals that remained unsold on the delivery date of the new stamps.

The government agreed to the deal. The 1881 stamps were demonetized, and Guatemala's railway tax stamps were surcharged for regular use until new stamps could be provided by Parker.

Eventually, the remaining stamps from the 1881 and provisional issues reached Calman, the New York stamp dealer. In his new acquisition, he discovered several sheets of the Small Quetzals with the centers inverted.

ABNC printed the stamps in two operations — the frames and the centers. During the second operation, a few sheets of the stamps were turned upside down, creating inverted centers.

In "The Postage Stamps of Guatemala," which was published in the *American Philatelist*, Bertram Poole said the first mention of the 2c invert appeared in the *Philatelic Record* for August 1882. He said Calman revealed the discovery of the 20c as early as 1888 in the *American Journal of Philately*.

Poole indicated that the 5c was unknown until one appeared at auction in New York in 1891. In the International Society of Guatemala Collectors' *Handbook of Guatemala Philately*, edited by Roland A. Goodman, it says the first mention of the 5c invert appeared in European philatelic papers in July 1887, and the discovery of the 20c error appeared in the same publication in August 1887. The handbook credits J.W. Scott of New York with reporting the discovery of the 2c invert in April 1888.

Of the three inverts, the 5c is the scarcest. Only one sheet is believed to ever have existed. According to the Guatemala handbook, only four unused copies have been reported, and only two of these have original gum. Count Ferrari, the famous French collector, owned one of the copies with original gum.

The handbook also says that the ISGC inventory shows 20 used copies of the 5c invert in members' collections. The only multiple of the 5c error is a used horizontal pair — a scarce item indeed.

A block of six and two blocks of four exist of the 20c invert. This error is more common than the 5c. Several sheets of the 2c escaped the printer. The largest known multiple is a block of 10.

Scott catalog prices these errors at $275 mint and $250 used for the 2c; $4,000 mint and $1,600 used for the 5c; and $350 mint and $325 used for the 20c. The 5c invert error is one of Guatemala's scarcest stamps.

Shortage or Surplus?

VALUE: $10,000 plus

This whaling cover to New Bedford is franked with five of the rare 1857 Hawaii 5¢-on-13¢ provisional stamps.

Hawaii claims several of the world's stamp rarities. Most famous of all, of course, are the Missionaries. A less famous, but scarce, Hawaiian stamp is the 5¢-on-13¢ provisional of 1857. This stamp has been the subject of disagreements between collectors.

For several years, it was believed to be a fake. However, in the 1940s, evidence was found to prove its authenticity. Collectors also have argued over whether the provisional was issued because of a shortage of 5¢ stamps or due to a surplus of 13¢ stamps.

In 1855, the United States letter rate to and from California was increased to 10¢. Prior to this increase, the 13¢ stamps covered the combined 5¢ Hawaiian rate and the 8¢ U.S. rate. Thus, when the U.S. rate was increased, the 13¢ stamps became obsolete.

In 1857, a shortage of 5¢ stamps necessitated the surcharging of the excess stocks of 13¢ stamps. The King Kamehameha III 13¢ stamps of 1853 were surcharged with a manuscript "5."

These surcharged stamps are extremely rare on cover, with fewer than a dozen known to exist. The late Alfred Caspary, the renowned American collector, owned half of these covers.

One is franked with the U.S. 1851-56 1¢ blue type II (Scott 7) and

U.S. 1851-56 10¢ green type III (Scott 15). The Scott U.S. Specialized catalog lists this cover, but gives no price.

Caspary also owned a cover with the 5¢ surcharge used with the U.S. 1851-56 10¢ green type II (Scott 14). Scott lists this cover at $15,000. The same price is given for a cover bearing the U.S. 1851-56 12¢ black (Scott 17). Two covers with this combination were owned by Caspary. One was from the Ferrari collection; the other from the Seybold collection. Scott lists other covers bearing the 5¢ provisional at $10,000.

A particularly impressive cover is franked with five singles of the 5¢ provisional used in combination with two of the U.S. 10¢ green stamps, one type II and the others type III, and the 12¢ black. This whaling cover, addressed to New Bedford, Massachusetts, sold for $8,500 in the Caspary sale conducted by H.R. Harmer of New York October 8-9, 1957. It was purchased by Ryohei Ishikawa, who also amassed the finest collection of classic U.S.

Ishikawa also purchased other covers carrying the 5¢-on-13¢ provisional. These were auctioned by Sotheby Parke Bernet in November 1980. Singles of this scarce provisional are listed in Scott at $4,500 mint and $5,500 used. A mint copy sold for $1,155, including a 10-percent buyer's premium, at the December 4-6, 1985, Richard Wolffers auction.

Appearance is Deceiving

VALUE: $825

What appears to be an Albany essay is actually an error from Ireland.

At first glance, the illustrated stamp appears to be a perforated Albany essay — a most peculiar item. However, it is not a United States stamp at all. It is a stamp from Ireland — the 1976 U.S. Bicentennial issue with the silver inscription missing.

Imagine the reaction of the collector who discovered this error when he purchased a sheet of 100 of the 15-penny U.S. Bicentennial stamp at a tiny post office in County Galway, Ireland.

The collector, a Canadian, was vacationing in Ireland. He continued his tour of the island, but before leaving the Emerald Isle, he stopped in to visit stamp dealer David Feldman in Dublin. The collector showed his find to Feldman, who made him an offer. Feldman bought the entire sheet.

Feldman exhibited a copy of the error at INTERPHIL '86, the international philatelic exhibition staged in Philadelphia. The error attracted attention not only because it was the first of its kind in the history of Irish stamps, but also because of its striking similarity to the Albany essay, especially since the country name was missing.

Ireland celebrated the bicentennial of the U.S. with four stamps and a souvenir sheet issued May 17, 1976. The 7-penny and 8p denominations were printed in ultramarine, silver and red, and featured the 50 stars and stripes. The 9p and 15p reproduced the

Albany essay. The 9p was printed in blue, silver and ocher; the 15p in red, silver and blue.

The Albany essay was produced by Gavit & Company in 1847 for a proposed Albany (New York) postmaster's provisional. It features a profile portrait of Benjamin Franklin with "ALBANY OFFICE" on either side and "POSTAGE/FIVE CENTS" at top and bottom. The essay itself is scarce.

Although the 7p Bicentennial stamp also exists with the silver inscription omitted, the error is not as striking as the 15p with the Albany essay standing alone. The normal 15p stamp features the essay along with the inscription "American Declaration of Independence 1776, Benjamin Franklin" in silver diagonally across the upper left portion of the stamps. Also in silver is "15 Eire" horizontally across the lower left corner.

The omission of the silver removes the issuing country's name, the value and the purpose for this issue, thus creating a stunning error. Scott and Stanley Gibbons catalogs list the missing-silver error on the 7p, 15p and miniature sheet, which repeats the four stamp designs from the set. Scott prices the 7p error at $250 used. The 15p is listed at $825 mint and $900 used. Scott does not price the missing-silver error on the minature sheet. However, the Mac-Donnell Whyte *Stamps of Ireland* catalog prices it at I£1,700 (about U.S. $2,500).

Manx Error of Color

VALUE: Indeterminable

The ocher border of the 1974 6-penny stamp appears in error on this 3p.

The stamps of Britain's island possessions seem to create problems for the Swiss printer Courvoisier SA.

Courvoisier's first printing error to find its way into a collector's hands was the Jersey 1969 10/- error of color. The background of this 10/- stamp, depicting the Royal Court, was printed in the green color of the 50-penny value, which featured the same design.

A few years later, a similar error of color was created — this time involving a stamp from Isle of Man.

Isle of Man is an island in the Irish Sea, west of Great Britain. As a self-governing crown possession, it used British stamps, along with its own regional issues after 1958. In July 1973, its postal administration separated from Britain and began issuing its own stamps.

Isle of Man's first set of definitive stamps depicts island scenes, historical places, and fauna indigenous to the island. Each stamp features a border in a different color carrying the Manx coat of arms, the inscription "ISLE OF MAN," and the value.

Not until more than a decade had passed did the error come to light. A collector discovered examples of the 3p definitive with the border printed in the ocher color of the 6p border rather than its normal green color. Alan Benjamin, owner of B. Alan Ltd., a British firm specializing in errors and varieties, said the collector discovered 10 panes of four showing this error. The panes are from booklets of these definitives released in 1974.

During the printing of the border on the 6p stamps, Courvoisier apparently fed a sheet of the 3p into the press, resulting in 3p stamps with the ocher border color of the 6p.

The error of color on the Jersey stamp was perhaps more forgivable because in that case both denominations showed the same designs. It is understandable that the printer could have mistaken the 10/- for the 50p. However, this is not the case with the Isle of Man error. The 3p shows the Douglas Promenade; the 6p features Cregneish Village.

The error not only slipped past the printer, but it also escaped detection by Courvoisier's eagle-eye inspectors.

Count Ferrari's Follies

VALUE: $10,000

This scarce 80c provisional of the Italian State of Modena is tied on piece by a blue double circular cancel.

Beginning stamp collectors sometimes snip stamps from covers, not realizing that some stamps are more valuable on cover than off. But it is difficult to imagine a prominent collector such as Count Ferrari being guilty of such action. During his lifetime (1858-1917), Ferrari amassed one of the world's greatest collections. He attempted to acquire an example of every stamp issued. He nearly achieved his goal.

Ferrari owned many of the world's great rarities, including the British Guiana 1¢ black on magenta of 1856. Yet, he had a quirk about extraneous paper in his collection. He frequently removed stamps from covers before adding the stamps to his collection. He lived to regret removing at least one stamp from its cover. This stamp was the 80-centesimo provisional issued by the Italian State of Modena in 1859.

Modena was ruled by Duke Francis V. In 1859, the duke was overthrown, and the duchy was annexed to the Kingdom of Sardinia. In the interim, the provisional government issued a set of stamps ranging in values from 5c to 80c. The stamps featured a common design showing the Cross of Savoy coat of arms.

The 80c denomination seldom saw use, which contributed to this stamp's scarcity in used condition. In his book, *Stamps of Great Price*, Nevile Stocken says Ferrari purchased a cover bearing this rarity from Hugo Griebert. The count immediately tore the stamp off the cover, mounted it in his collection, and discarded the "extraneous" paper.

Later, he learned that while this stamp is scarce in used condition off cover, it is extremely rare on cover. Today, Scott catalog lists this provisional at $10,000 used. Mint copies are priced at only $60. Count Ferrari must have learned his lesson with this Modena stamp because he later added several scarce covers to his collection with stamps intact.

Stocken also mentions a cover bearing a strip of three of the 80c, with the right-hand stamp showing the error "CENT. 8." instead of "CENT. 80." The cover was addressed to Messrs. Viti Brothers in Philadelphia.

Alfred Caspary, who acquired many rarities in the early years of the 20th century, owned an example of the 80c on piece. The provisional is tied by a blue double circular cancel inscribed "GUASTALLA/21/GENNAJO/1860."

Sardinia became part of the Kingdom of Italy in 1861, and Italian stamps came into use in this region.

The Abolitionists' Rarity

VALUE: $16,000

Jamaica's scarce unissued 1921 6-penny Abolition of Slavery stamp.

Two rarities came out of Jamaica's 1919-21 definitive series. One is the well-known 1-shilling Statue of Queen Victoria stamp with the inverted frame. The other is a lesser known 6-penny stamp. This rarity was never issued.

In 1921, Jamaica planned the release of the 6d definitive marking the abolition of slavery. It showed the gathering in the square at Spanish Town on August 1, 1836, when Sir Lionel Smith, Jamaica's governor, read the declaration of freedom from slavery.

Just prior to its release in June 1921, the release of the stamp was canceled due to political unrest on the island. The government feared the subject of the stamp would be used as propaganda to encourage unrest among the blacks. The Jamaican Post Office ordered a new supply of the King George V 6d to be used until a different design could be created. Later in 1922, a 6d was released showing Port Royal in 1853.

The 6d Abolition of Slavery stamp was canceled so close to the proposed issue date that stocks of the stamps already were on the island. The post office burned these supplies. Crown Agents in London, who coordinated Jamaica's stamps, also ordered its stocks destroyed.

The Jamaican Post Office kept one block of four of the unissued stamp for its archives. Another block was given to King George V for the Royal Collection. The only other examples of this stamp which were not destroyed were those which had been overprinted "SPECIMEN" and were distributed by the Universal Postal Union.

The Jamaican Post Office archival block eventually disappeared. Single stamps from this block have been discovered. In his *Jamaica: A Review of the Nations's Postal History and Postage*, published in 1964, Alfred N. Johnson said one example from this block was in England, another in Ireland, and two in the United States.

Christie's/Robson Lowe sold one of these copies for £10,800 (about $16,000) in its January 22, 1986, auction. The stamp had been part of the Jamaica collection of a prominent U.S. collector.

"SPECIMEN" copies of this stamp sell for much less than those without the overprint. Two specimens sold in the January 22, 1986, Christie's/Robson Lowe sale for £129 ($190) and £259 ($390). In a footnote, Scott catalog lists stamps without the "SPECIMEN" overprint at $20,000 and those with the overprint at $1,250.

Earthquakes Take Toll

VALUE: $22,500
This 1874 20 sen with syllabic character 1 was in the Caspary collection.

Two earthquakes contributed to the scarcity of a Japanese issue. Five examples of this rarity were recorded; only four exist today. One was destroyed in an earthquake. Another survived an earthquake but was badly damaged.

In January 1874, Japan began adding Katakana syllabic characters to its stamps. The stamps show the chrysanthemum crest featured on many of the early Japanese issues.

The syllabic characters have been the subject of much debate. Some collectors compared the characters to plate numbers. However, A.M. Tracey Woodward, the foremost authority on Japanese stamps, said in his book, *The Postage Stamps of Japan and Dependencies*, that the syllabic characters actually were controls.

Woodward said, "These syllabics, in short, were not plate numbers at all, but were intended to serve as check marks during a short-lived attempt at organized control of the sale of stamps, which never fulfilled its mission nor realized the results expected of it simply because it was never methodically carried out." He said this is shown, for example, in the "irregular quantity issued one syllabic character, as compared to others."

One of Japan's great philatelic rarities is part of this issue — the 1874 20-sen red violet with syllabic figure 1. The 20s with syllabic figure 1 exists only with a specimen (mihon) dot. It is listed in a footnote in Scott catalog and priced at $22,500.

For many years, only three copies of this stamp were known, all unused. One was in the J.H. Crocker collection.

In 1906, an earthquake, and subsequent fire, devastated San Francisco. Huge forces ripped apart buildings. Fire swept the city, taking about 700 lives. Property damage was estimated at $425 million, an amount which included several of the world's great stamp rarities housed in the Crocker collection. Among these rarities was the Japan 20s with the syllabic character.

Crocker also owned one of the greatest Hawaiian collections at that time. Fortunately, most of this collection was being displayed at an international stamp exhibition in London at the time of the earthquake.

The second copy of the Japanese rarity was in the Stoltz collection. This copy was acquired by Alfred Caspary. The stamp realized $3,600 at the Caspary sales conducted by H.R. Harmer of New York in 1958.

The third copy was in the Woodward collection. In 1917, Woodward was offered more than $1,000 for the stamp — an offer he refused. The offer was much publicized in the philatelic press and resulted in the discovery of a fourth copy a year later.

The fourth copy was purchased by Mr. Fujio of Kamakura, Japan. Ironically, it nearly suffered the same fate as the Crocker copy. A tidal wave flooded Fujio's home in Kamakura, following an earthquake in 1923. Fujio rescued his collection, but the 20s stamp was badly damaged by sea water.

A fifth copy of the Japanese rarity, also badly damaged, was discovered in the H.G. Fletcher collection in 1927.

Although not as scarce as the 20s with syllabic figure 1, the 20s with syllabic figures 2 and 3 are expensive. Scott catalog lists the syllabic figure 2 stamp at $7,500 and syllabic figure 3 at $7,250.

Courvoisier's first mistake

VALUE: $3,500

Jersey's 10-shilling color error was
the first to slip through Courvoisier.

Jersey's 1969 10-shilling error of color has the distinction of being the first error produced by the reputable Swiss printing firm, Courvoisier SA. In 1969, the Channel Island of Jersey gained its postal independence from Great Britain and began issuing its own stamps. The low values were produced by Harrison & Sons in England; the high values were printed by Courvoisier.

This set was short-lived since Great Britain and the Channel Islands converted from pounds, shillings and pence to decimal currency on February 15, 1971.

The decimal definitives carried the same designs as the first set. Only the values and background colors changed. The 10-penny, 20p and 50p stamps featured the same designs as the 2/6d, 5/- and 10/-, respectively.

While Courvoisier was printing the new stamps, the Jersey Post Office also ordered the reprinting of the still current 10/- which showed the Royal Court. During this reprinting, the printer slipped up. One sheet of 25 inadvertently was fed into the press which was set up to produce the green background of the 50p stamp. The 50p also showed the Royal Court, which accounts for the mistake.

The result was that a sheet of 10/- stamps, which normally carried a gray background, was mistakenly produced with a green background. What was more surprising than the error itself was that it slipped through the elaborate security controls of Courvoisier. It remained undetected, or at least was not publicized, until 1972. That year it was sold to the British new-issue dealer Urch, Harris and Company.

The sheet has since been broken up. In October 1972, a single copy was auctioned in England. It realized £260. Today, Scott catalog lists the error at $3,500.

'Un Pranc' for 'Un Franc'

VALUE: $6,750 plus

The left-hand stamp carries the rare "Un Pranc" error.
The normal surcharge appears on the right-hand stamp.

A spelling error occurred during the overprinting of Luxembourg stamps in 1879. The word "Franc" appears as "Pranc" on a few copies of the 1-franc-on-37½-centime stamp.

In 1872, following the Franco-Prussian War, Luxembourg signed a new postal convention with Germany. This permitted letters of declared values to pass between the two countries. In his book, *The Postal History of the Grand Duchy of Luxembourg*, Francis Rhein explains that in addition to the ordinary postal rate, a fee equal to that imposed on registered letters was charged for these letters. Also, an insurance premium of ½ silbergroschen per 20 thaler was added. Rhein says these letters had to be closed with five seals, and their prepayment was compulsory.

The Luxembourg postal administration decided to issue a higher-denomination stamp (1fr) to be used on these letters. The 37½c stamp of the 1865-74 issue had seen little use. Today this value without the overprint is one of the scarcest stamps of Luxembourg.

The postal administration decided to surcharge the seldom-used 37½c with a 1fr value. In 1873, a number of the 37½c stamps were surcharged locally with "Un Franc" in black.

In 1879, the 37½c stamp again was surcharged with the 1fr value, this time by Pierre Bruck, another printer in Luxembourg. The rare "Un Pranc" surcharge occurs twice on each sheet produced during this overprinting. The spelling error probably was made just once, not twice, by Bruck. Its appearance twice in a sheet results from the surcharge being set 50 times in five rows of 10, and then being applied twice to the sheet of 100 stamps.

During the 1879 overprinting, 1,042 sheets received the surcharge. Since the error occurred twice on each sheet, it can be concluded that 2,084 errors were produced.

But the postal administration discovered the error before most of the sheets could be released to the public. It ordered the stamps with the error removed from the sheets and destroyed. A few copies escaped detection and were sold to the public. These are scarce, particularly in used condition.

Scott catalog lists the error at $5,500 mint and $6,750 used. The most impressive example of this error is a used horizontal pair with the left-hand stamp showing the incorrect "Pranc" surcharge and the right-hand copy showing the normal surcharge. The pair carries an Echternach town cancel.

Orange 'Hanging Hair'

VALUE: $9,000

The Netherlands' controversial 5¢
Hanging Hair orange error of color.

Is the 1894 5¢ orange error of color of the Netherlands a rarity or a fraud? Collectors of Dutch stamps have raised this question several times. Yet, the stamp continues to bring high prices at auction, and major stamp catalogs continue to list the error. Scott catalog prices it at $9,000 mint, $6,750 used.

The Netherlands issued a 5¢ blue stamp, portraying Queen Wilhelmina, as part of its 1891-94 series. These stamps are known as the "Hanging Hair" issue. Shortly after the 5¢ blue stamp's release, copies appeared in orange.

For nearly 100 years, the 5¢ orange has been regarded as one of the Netherlands' great rarities. Some collectors say the stamp is an error of color. Others say it is likely the "error" is from a proof sheet that accidently was sent to the post office. The postal clerk mistook the sheet for the 3¢ orange and sold about 50 copies of the stamp before noticing the error. The remaining copies were withdrawn from sale and returned to the postal officials.

Other collectors condemn the 5¢ orange as a fraud. Gert Holstege, in the Dutch journal *Het Maandblad voor Philatelie*, presented what he said is conclusive evidence that the "error" was produced deliberately by a foreman at the printing plant of Joh. Enschede & Zonen.

Holstege's article was reprinted in the June 1984 and September 1984 issues of *Netherlands Philately*, the journal of the American Society for Netherlands Philately. He quoted reports by B.J.R. Engelbregt, who was chief of the first division of the Central Direction of Posts and Telegraphs of the Netherlands at the time the stamp was produced.

According to the reports, Carl Gietzelt, a foreman at Joh. Enschede, discovered he could produce extra sheets of stamps by having them printed on unmarked paper and having them removed from the factory before they could be discovered. He used these stamps to make purchases. For example, Engelbregt said Gietzelt bought a bottle of cognac with stamps produced in this manner.

Then the idea struck Gietzelt. He could make even more money by selling "errors." He ordered the printing of the 5¢ stamp in orange instead of the normal blue, thus creating the orange "error of color." According to Holstege's research, the foreman sold a few copies to collectors and dealers. Others were given to people in payment of goods (perhaps another bottle of cognac). A few of these were mistaken as 3¢ stamps, which were printed in orange, and placed on letters.

The post office caught on to Gietzelt's shenanigans. Engelbregt brought it to the attention of Joh. Enschede. A private investigation was conducted, and Gietzelt was fired.

Holstege concludes that the 5¢ orange is not a postage stamp or a proof. It is a fraud, he says. Not all collectors agree. In a later issue of *Het Maandblad voor Philatelie*, Dutch philatelist Roelf Boekema says that Holstege's research dispels much of the mystery behind this fascinating stamp. However, Boekema feels that since the stamps were used to frank mail, the forgery was intended to defraud the post office, not the collector.

And so the questions continue. Is this stamp a gem or a fraud? Will the new evidence diminish collectors' interest in the stamp, or will the publicity help increase its value? Only time will tell.

The Priceless Queen

VALUE: $12,500

This No. 8 margin copy of the Netherlands 1928 9¢ Queen Wilhelmina issue shows the value-omitted error in a pair with the normal stamp.

A baroness discovered one of the Netherlands' scarcest stamps — the 1928 9¢ missing value. In the late 1920s, the baroness entered the Dutch post office in Het Loo and purchased a sheet of 200 of the 9¢ Queen Wilhelmina stamp from the 1926-39 series.

She noticed something peculiar about the first vertical row of stamps on the sheet. Each carried a blank box at the bottom of the stamp where the value should have been.

This is the only recorded sheet with the value omitted. The sheet eventually was broken up. Each error was left attached to a normal 9¢ value. Of course, none of these was used on mail.

How did this error occur? The rotary printing of this issue required two passes through the press — one for the orange red color and one for the black value. The first row of 20 in the sheet was printed last. During the printing of the sheet, the press was stopped before this row received the black printing, thus omitting the value.

Of the 20 copies of the error, two are in the Netherlands Postal Museum. Collectors and dealers own the remaining 18. Scott catalog prices this error at $12,500.

Through Nazi Hands

VALUE: $6,500

At left is shown a used copy of the Dutch 10¢-on-2½¢ European PTT issue with surcharge omitted. The normal surcharged copy is shown at right.

Nazi Germany greatly influenced the Dutch stamp issuing policy during the occupation of the Netherlands. By 1942, Dutch stamps reflected German ideals. That year, a pair of semipostals was issued honoring the Netherlands Legion which was incorporated into the Waffen SS.

A set of 1943-44 definitives featured old Germanic symbols and Dutch naval heroes, who defeated the British in the 17th century.

Most of the stamps issued during this period are common, but one rarity does exist. On January 15, 1943, the Netherlands issued a stamp to commemorate the founding of the European Union of Posts and Telegraphs on October 19, 1942. The union was formed by the German puppet governments in Europe. Many of these governments issued stamps to honor the union.

For the occasion, the Netherlands Post Office surcharged an unissued 2½¢ Posthorn stamp with a 10¢ value. The surcharge reads: "EUROPEESCHE/P T T/VEREENIGING/19 OCTOBER 1942/ 10 CENT."

The 2½¢ stamp never was issued without the surcharge, but a few copies with the surcharge omitted escaped the printer and probably found their way into the hands of the Nazis. Today, these unoverprinted stamps are among the great philatelic rarities of the Netherlands.

Only 20 copies exist — 14 unused and six used. Scott catalog prices missing-surcharge copies at $6,000 unused and $6,500 used. This compares to 8¢ and 25¢ for the surcharged copies. A mint copy of the missing-surcharge stamp sold for $4,400, including a 10-percent buyer's premium, at John Kaufmann's December 6, 1985, auction.

South Pacific Error

VALUE: $11,000

The top stamp of this New Hebrides
vertical pair is missing the overprint.

New Hebrides (now Vanuatu) always has been a fascinating country, both historically and philatelically. Pedro de Queiros, a Portuguese explorer, discovered these Pacific islands in 1606. Captain James Cook, the famous British explorer, reached the is-

113

lands in 1774.

The French, who ruled nearby New Caledonia, began to gain power in New Hebrides. Following several years of discontent on the islands, the Condominium Treaty was signed in 1906, providing for the joint rule of the New Hebrides by the British and French.

This joint rule also was reflected in the postage stamps of the islands. The first series of stamps was released in 1908, when the Condominium officially was established. French stamps were overprinted for use by the French nationals. Because the British high commissioner in the New Hebrides also was governor of Fiji, Fijian stamps were overprinted for use by the British nationals.

The scarcest stamp of the New Hebrides is an error from this overprinted series of Fijian stamps. The Government Printing Establishment in Suva, Fiji, overprinted the Fiji Edward VII keyplate issues for use in the New Hebrides. The stamps were overprinted "NEW HEBRIDES/CONDOMINIUM" in two lines. However, during the overprinting, the printer failed to strike several stamps. This resulted in se-tenant vertical pairs with one stamp showing the overprint and the other with the overprint omitted.

In their book, *The New Hebrides: Their Postal History and Postage Stamps*, Nathan Hals and Phil Collas say the first mention of these errors was in the September 1911 *Gibbons Monthly Journal*. In the journal, E.B. Powers showed a block of 42 of the New Hebrides overprints with the top row of six missing the overprint.

In 1935, H.R. Harmer of London sold a vertical pair with the upper stamp missing the overprint. In 1939, the same company offered a block of ten with the fourth stamp down showing the omitted overprint variety.

Today, pairs showing the missing overprint realize high prices when sold. In its January 30, 1986, auction, Colonial Stamp Company offered a vertical pair with the top stamp missing the overprint. It realized $11,000, including a 10-percent buyer's premium. Scott catalog lists these errors at $8,000. Only mint copies exist.

Caribou For 50¢

VALUE: $18,700

One of only five recorded blocks of four of Newfoundland's 50¢-on-36¢ "Columbia" airmail issue of 1930.

Newfoundland is famous for its provisional airmail stamps issued in the early 1900s for pioneer flights. Collectors are familiar with Newfoundland's first airmail stamp, the overprint used for the Hawker/Grieve first transatlantic attempt, and the scarce De Pinedo overprints. A lesser known, yet interesting airmail provisional is the "Columbia" surcharge of 1930.

In September 1930, Captain Errol Boyd and his navigator, Lieutenant Harry P. Connor, arrived at the Harbour Grace Airport in Newfoundland in the Bellanca monoplane *Columbia* to begin their transatlantic flight to London, England.

Boyd agreed to carry mail on the second flight. The Newfoundland Post Office authorized a special stamp for the occasion. The post office surcharged its 36¢ Caribou stamp with the inscription, "Trans-Atlantic/AIR MAIL/B. M./'Columbia'/September/1930/-Fifty Cents." The initials "B. M." stood for "Bellanca Monoplane."

D. Thistle at the *Royal Gazette*, the local newspaper, surcharged this airmail issue. In *The Postage Stamps and Postal History of Newfoundland*, author Winthrop S. Boggs says the surcharge setting consisted of four subjects. The first line was linotyped; the remaining six were typeset.

Each of the four subjects have different characteristics, making it easy for collectors to plate this issue. Boggs explains that three sheets of the 36¢ Caribou stamp were broken into blocks of four, and the 75 pieces were put through the press.

On September 25, an announcement appeared in the Newfoundland press that 160 letters would be carried on *Columbia*. (Actually, 300 were accepted.) At 9 a.m. September 25, the post office placed 252 of the 300 surcharged stamps on sale at the St. John's General Post Office. Forty-eight were sold at Harbour Grace.

The postal clerks affixed each stamp to the envelopes. All St. John's mail bearing this issue was canceled September 25. Boggs says 110 of the stamps sold at St. John's and all those sold at Harbour Grace were used on letters.

Captain Boyd and Lieutenant Connor took off from Harbour Grace October 9 carrying 100 pieces of mail franked with the surcharged stamps and 230 pieces franked with ordinary stamps. The *Columbia* was forced to land the following day on the beach at Tresco Island. From there, it continued its journey to its final destination, Croydon Airport in London.

Only five blocks of four of the "Columbia" surcharge exist. One block was sold in the 1986 Robert A. Siegel Rarities sale for $18,700. Two mint singles sold for $2,800 and $1,900 in the same sale. A single brought £1,760 (about $2,465) at the Harmers of London March 11-12, 1986, auction of the "Pegasus" airmail collection. Scott catalog lists this issue at $8,000 mint and used.

DO-X Inverted Surcharges

VALUE: $12,000

Only 20 copies of Newfoundland's 1932 Dornier DO-X airmail stamp with the surcharge inverted are recorded.

The Newfoundland Post Office surcharged 8,000 stamps in 1932 for the Dornier DO-X flight. Twenty exist with an inverted surcharge. These invert errors number among the world's great airmail rarities.

Germany began experimental flights with the giant flying boat, Dornier DO-X, in 1929. In 1930, the DO-X set out on its maiden transoceanic voyage, from Friedrichschafen, Germany, to South America. It then flew to the United States and on to Newfoundland, arriving at Holyrood on May 20, 1932.

Covers exist for these flights, but for stamp collectors, the most famous flight of the DO-X flying boat was from Newfoundland to Germany in May 1932. It was for this flight that special stamps were created. On May 19, the Newfoundland Post Office announced that it would sell specially surcharged stamps to be used on mail carried on the DO-X flight. Only 3,000 covers were permitted to be carried on the flight.

Appropriately, the Newfoundland Post Office used its 1931 $1 airmail stamp, showing routes of historic transatlantic flights, to create an issue for the DO-X flight. The $1 stamp was surcharged in red, "TRANS-ATLANTIC/WEST TO EAST/Per Dornier DO-X/May,

1932./One Dollar and Fifty Cents." The original $1 denomination on the stamp was obliterated with a solid line.

The sale of these $1.50-on-$1 stamps was limited to four per customer. In *The Postage Stamps and Postal History of Newfoundland*, author Winthrop Boggs says the 8,000 surcharged stamps were sold out May 19, the first day of issue.

While these stamps are fascinating both on and off cover, the true gems are those sporting the inverted surcharge. The printer, D.R. Thistle and Company, surcharged the special stamps in a setting of four. The sheets of $1 stamps were broken up into blocks of four for the surcharging. Apparently, the printer turned five blocks upside down while feeding them into the press to apply the surcharge. This resulted in inverted surcharges.

Collectors eagerly seek copies of this rarity. None was used to frank mail carried on the DO-X flight; only used examples exist. Scott catalog prices these errors at $12,000.

Stamp Packet Rarities

VALUE: $1,820

The overprint was omitted on the bottom 1¢ stamp of this vertical pair.

Collectors at the Malaya-Borneo Exhibition in 1922 were unaware that the packets they purchased at the Borneo building could contain rarities. The Malaya-Borneo Exhibition, a trade show organized by the governments of the Federated Malay States, Straits Settlements, British North Borneo, Brunei and Sarawak, opened in Singapore March 31, 1922.

The participating countries overprinted contemporary stamps with an inscription honoring the exhibition. North Borneo overprinted its 1909-22 engraved definitives and its 1911 25¢ and 50¢. The overprint reads in three lines in red or blue: "MALAYA-BORNEO/EXHIBITION/1922."

The North Borneo stamps sold at the exhibition were available only in packets. These packets contained one, five or ten sets. When they opened the packets, collectors found they contained a variety of stamps ranging from badly torn copies, damaged by careless postal clerks, to examples of overprint errors.

Most of these errors were spelling mistakes: ''BORHEO,'' ''BORNEQ,'' ''EXHIBITICN'' and ''MILAYA.'' Stanley Gibbons catalog prices for these errors range from £13 to £1,750. A vertical pair of the 1¢ with one stamp missing the overprint catalogs at £1,000. An example was sold in the March 5-6, 1986, auction conducted by

VALUE: $1,690

One of only 10 copies of the 1922
16¢ overprinted in red instead of blue.

Gibbons' Hong Kong branch for HK$14,000 (about U.S. $1,820).

The most celebrated of these errors, however, is the 16¢ stamp overprinted in red. The overprint on this value normally was blue. A Chinese banker discovered a strip of five of this error in the packet he purchased at the exhibition.

Unaware of the scarcity of his find, the banker exchanged one copy with a Singapore collector, Dr. Tan Bin Cheang, for a copy of the 20¢ overprinted in red. Only 10 copies of the 16¢ overprinted in red have been recorded. The Gibbons' catalog lists the stamp at £2,000. At the March 1986 Gibbons Hong Kong auction, a copy realized HK$13,000 (about U.S. $1,690).

Prices do not reflect the scarcity of these errors. This is due, in part, to the unpopularity of the exhibition issues from their inception. Collectors took offense to these issues, feeling they were unnecessary and excessive. At first, stamp catalog editors refused to list them. Scott catalog was among the last to recognize the stamps, although they were valid for postage.

Scott has listed the stamps for several years now, yet the catalog still does not recognize the errors. Were they created as philatelic curiosities? The postmaster of North Borneo at the time said they were not. He said the errors were the result of a rushed printing job. The printers were given only a few days to overprint the stamps. Whether the errors were the result of carelessness or hanky-panky is subject to conjecture.

Cape to the Rescue

VALUE: $10,000

Both 4d stamps in this pair feature the overprint with "COMPANY" omitted. The overprint should read "BRITISH/SOUTH AFRICA/COMPANY.

Several rarities exist among the provisional stamps created during the Matabele uprising in Bulawayo in Rhodesia (now Zimbabwe). On March 24, 1896, the Matabele tribe rebelled against the British South Africa Company, which controlled Rhodesia at that time.

Bulawayo was cut off from Salisbury, the postal headquarters of the country. The supply of stamps in Bulawayo dwindled. To make matters worse, a mailcoach carrying a supply of stamps to the town was ambushed, and the stamps were stolen. Postal authorities in Bulawayo were forced to create provisional issues.

In April 1896, the local printer, Philpott & Collins, who also printed the town newspaper, *Bulawayo Chronicle*, surcharged the 3-penny and 4-shilling 1890-94 British South Africa issues with the inscription, "One Penny," in black with three bars below.

Philpott & Collins was inexperienced in stamp production. As could be expected, errors occurred. Some are extremely rare. The 1d-on-3d and 1d-on-4/- both are known with the "P" of "Penny" inverted. Scott lists the 1d-on-3d and the 1d-on-4/- errors with the "P" inverted at $12,500 unused. The 1d-on-4/- also has been found with a single bar surcharge instead of the normal three bars. Scott lists this at $2,000 unused.

Another scarce error on this stamp shows an inverted "y" in "Penny." It is priced in Scott at $12,500. A few sheets of the 5/- 1890-94 stamps were surcharged "THREE/PENCE" in two lines with bars below. This issue is found with the "T" or "R" of "THREE" inverted. Scott lists these varieties at $20,000.

In addition to these rarities, the basic surcharged issues, without varieties, are expensive because these provisionals were seldom sold over the counter. To protect against speculation, letters had to be handed in at the post office. The stamps were affixed by postal clerks. An exception was made, however, if it could be determined the provisionals would be used for revenue purposes on receipts. In this case, individuals could purchase a maximum of six provisionals.

Although Bulawayo was cut off from its main stamp supplier in Salisbury, it did maintain communication with Cape Town in the Cape of Good Hope. In early May, all stocks of stamps in Bulawayo were depleted. The postal officials in the town contacted the post office in Cape Town and requested a supply of Cape of Good Hope stamps to be overprinted for use in Rhodesia.

These stamps were sent to Bulawayo as requested. Cape of Good Hope stamps in denominations of ½d, 1d, 2d, 3d, 4d, 6d and 1/- were overprinted "BRITISH/SOUTH AFRICA/COMPANY" in three lines in black. They were placed on sale May 22.

The rarity among these overprinted issues is the 4d with "COM-PANY" omitted. Scott lists this error at $16,000 unused. A mint horizontal pair with both stamps missing "COMPANY" realized £6,264 (about U.S. $10,000) at the Christie's/Robson Lowe auction in London June 10, 1986. Colonial Stamp Company sold a single for $11,500, including the 10-percent buyer's premium, at its December 1, 1986, auction. Forgeries of these surcharged and overprinted issues are numerous.

Georgia's Favor Bisects

VALUE: $20,000

Russia's Kutais bisect, consisting of the lower right half of the stamp, appears on this envelope to Telaw.

Seldom does an issue created especially for collectors command high prices. Collectors usually rebuke these philatelically oriented issues. However, two provisionals of Imperial Russia command five-figure prices when sold, even though their origin is believed to be purely philatelic.

These provisional issues are bisects of the Russian 1883-88 14-kopeck Posthorn issue. Bisects are stamps cut into two parts, with each part paying postage equal to half the face value of the complete stamp.

Many countries have used bisects as provisionals to overcome a shortage of stamps. However, collectors usually recognize only those bisects which are authorized by the post office and which serve a true need.

The bisects of the 1883-88 Russian 14kop are an exception. They met no such need; yet, collectors pay high prices to obtain these so-called provisionals. These bisects are handstamped "7." The 14kop stamp was cut in half diagonally, and the surcharge was applied in red.

These provisionals exist with cancellations of Kutais and Tiflis, both towns in the Russian region of Georgia. As far as Russian specialists have been able to determine, these 7kop bisects alleviated no shortage of stamps. It is believed they were issued by

VALUE: $20,000

The 7-kopeck bisect, tied by the Tiflis cancel, is shown on this cover, which was once in the Faberge collection.

postmasters of these regions to satisfy a prominent local collector with a lot of clout.

The cover bearing the Kutais provisional and addressed to Telaw is unique. The bisect, consisting of the lower right half of the stamp, is tied to a large envelope by the Kutais cancel. This remarkable rarity was in the Curie and Baughman collections before passing into the hands of Russian specialist Norman D. Epstein.

125

Epstein also owned a large part of a cover bearing the upper left half of the 14kop stamp surcharged "7." This bisect is tied by a Tiflis August 31, 1884, cancel. This piece was once in the Faberge collection.

Neither item sold when the Epstein collection was auctioned October 15-16, 1985, by Harmers of New York. Scott catalog lists these rarities at $20,000, proving that despite the speculative nature of these bisects, collectors overcome their biases to recognize the scarcity of these provisionals.

Stamps to the Rescue

VALUE: $7,000

St. Helena's 1960 Tristan Relief set ranks among the modern stamp rarities. The set was issued to aid victims of the volcanic eruption on Tristan.

The Commonwealth Office in London stirred up controversy in the stamp world in 1985 when it forbade the British Virgin Islands to release its Michael Jackson stamps because the queen's portrait also appeared on the set. According to protocol, the queen cannot be portrayed on a stamp honoring a living person other than members of the royal family.

But this was not the first time stamp collecting has been affected by a decision of the Commonwealth Office. In 1961, the office ordered the withdrawal of a set of stamps already issued, creating a set of modern rarities.

On October 9, 1961, a volcano erupted on Tristan da Cunha, a group of British islands in the South Atlantic midway between South America and southern Africa. People living on Tristan da Cunha Island were forced to evacuate to Great Britain. They did not return until 1963.

Tristan da Cunha is a dependency of St. Helena. Feeling responsible for the islanders, the St. Helena Post Office issued a set of relief stamps. The post office overprinted four values of Tristan's 1960 Fish definitives with "ST. HELENA/Tristan Relief."

The stamps were surcharged with the sterling equivalent of their decimal values: 2½¢+3 pence, 5¢+6d, 7½¢+9d and 10¢+1 shilling. They were sold at double face value to raise money for the homeless islanders.

The St. Helena Post Office released the semipostals October 12. However, when news of the relief stamps reached the Commonwealth Office, it ordered the post office to withdraw the stamps immediately since they had not been authorized by the London office. The post office complied with the order and withdrew the stamps from sale October 19, only a week after their release. All remaining stock was destroyed.

In the one-week period, only 434 sets of these stamps were sold. Thus, St. Helena's Tristan Relief quartet joined the ranks of the world's modern stamp rarities. Scott catalog lists this set at $7,000 mint and $2,750 used.

Steve Ivy auctioned two sets at the AMERIPEX international stamp show on May 26, 1986. One lightly hinged, original gum set realized $2,970. The other lot, a matched used set of bottom left corner blocks with first-day cancel, sold for $4,510. Both prices include a 10-percent buyer's premium. Cherrystone Stamp Auctions sold a set for $3,850, including a 10-percent buyer's premium, at its December 3-4, 1986, auction.

Key to the Commonwealth

VALUE: $8,625

Only one copy exists of the St. Vincent 1871-78 1/- vermilion, perf 15.

Mention St. Vincent to today's collector, and he immediately thinks of the Caribbean island now famous for its proliferation of new issues and Leaders of the World stamps featuring kings, queens, automobiles, locomotives and other unrelated topics.

Unfortunately, many new collectors do not realize that several early issues of St. Vincent are key stamps to a comprehensive British Commonwealth collection. Some also are great rarities.

One such rarity is the 1871-78 1-shilling vermilion, perforated 15. Only one copy of this stamp exists. It is used and has a small closed tear at the base.

J.L. Messenger, who compiled probably the greatest collection of St. Vincent in the world, found the 1/- vermilion in 1957.

Why is this stamp so scarce? In *St. Vincent* by A.D. Pierce, J.L. Messenger and Robson Lowe, the authors suggest that only one row or possibly one sheet of the 1/- was perforated on the Perkins,

Bacon "C" perforating machine (perf 15) before the operator resumed use of the "B" machine (perf 11-13), which was normally used for this value.

Of course, this raises the possibility of other existing copies. But where are they? The *St. Vincent* book sets the date of issue in 1878 because the handstamp on the stamp did not come into use until about September of that year. Scott catalog lists the year of issue as 1877.

The 1/- vermilion can be compared to the British Guiana penny magenta in scarcity, but not in value. The St. Vincent gem realized $8,625, including a 15-percent buyer's commission, at the David Feldman November 19-23, 1985, auction in New York City. The stamp was purchased by Colonial Stamp Company of Los Angeles. Scott catalog lists the 1/- at $25,000.

In 1980, the British Guiana penny magenta sold for a record $935,000, including a 10-percent buyer's commission. So the St. Vincent rarity hasn't come close to reaching the penny magenta in status or price. Nevertheless, it is St. Vincent's No. 1 rarity and truly ranks among the world's great stamps.

The 1/- vermilion also exists imperforate, although collectors question its status. The authors of the *St. Vincent* book say the imperforates tend to have the characteristics of a variety of the perf 15 stamp.

Scott catalog does not recognize the imperforates. Stanley Gibbons catalog lists them as varieties of the perf 15 and prices them at £1,800. Three copies exist, all in used condition. One is in the Royal Collection in Buckingham Palace.

Normal is Uncommon

VALUE: $15,000

*This Samoan "1 shilling" surcharge
is scarcer than the "1 shillings" error.*

To a non-collector, one of the most unusual characteristics of a stamp collector is his never-ending search for errors. In most other fields, a defect or error makes an item less valuable, not more valuable. But stamp collectors continue their quest for errors, believing these errors increase the stamp's value.

However, there is at least one case where this is not true. The 1914 1-shilling surcharge of Samoa is an example of an error being more common than the correct surcharge.

Samoa, or Western Samoa as it is called today, is an archipelago in the South Pacific, east of Fiji. (Six islands of the Samoan group became a territory of the United States in 1899 by treaty with Germany and Great Britain. These are known as American Samoa.)

Western Samoa was a German colony from 1899 until 1914. In 1914, following the outbreak of World War I, New Zealand troops seized the islands for Great Britain. The German colonial stamps were demonetized. Confiscated stocks of the contemporary issue, showing the kaiser's yacht *Hohenzollern*, were surcharged with the equivalent sterling denominations. The stamps also were overprinted "G.R.I." (Georgius Rex Imperator).

During the surcharging of the high values, only the value was altered. The word "shillings" remained in place. The result was the incorrect surcharge "1 shillings" on the 1-mark stamp. The plural was used for the currency instead of the singular "shilling."

One hundred 1m stamps were surcharged with the "1 shillings" inscription before the error was discovered. However, when it was finally corrected, only 35 copies were properly surcharged "1 shilling." So, the number of incorrectly surcharged stamps is about three times greater than the correctly surcharged issues.

According to Robson Lowe's *The Encyclopaedia of British Empire Postage Stamps*, Volume IV, the surcharged copies were few in number because these stamps were to be used only when necessary on mail. They were not to be sold to collectors. Of course, a few fortunate collectors managed to place copies in their albums.

Unused copies of the correct "1 shilling" on 1m are extremely rare. Scott catalog lists this issue at $15,000 unused and $10,000 used. Phillips in Great Britain auctioned a mint copy of this stamp at its April 2-3, 1987, sale. Scott lists the "1 shillings" stamp at $5,000 unused and $4,500 used.

Surcharge Upon Surcharge

VALUE: $10,450

Few copies exist of Straits Settlements 4¢-on-4¢-on-5¢ issue of 1884.

The Straits Settlements 1884 4¢-on-4¢-on-5¢ surcharge puzzled collectors for many years. Few copies existed; all were used. Collectors were familiar with the similar 8¢-on-8¢-on-12¢ surcharged issue. These stamps were common.

In the 1880s, the postal authorities of the Straits Settlements ordered the surcharging of several of its stamps. Among the stamps surcharged were the 5¢ and 12¢ denominations. The 5¢ was surcharged "4/Cents" in black or red; the 12¢ was surcharged "8/Cents" in black or blue. These surcharges were so faint that they were barely distinguishable.

The post office then ordered the 8¢-on-12¢ stamps surcharged with an additional large "8" in red.

In his study of the Straits Settlements, the late Dr. F.E. Wood said that philatelist W.A. Bicknell visited Singapore in 1913 to try to solve the mystery of the 4¢-on-4¢-on-5¢ stamp, which had similarly been surcharged with a large "4" in red. He visited the Government Printing Office, where the superintendent supplied him with a print, pulled in black, of numerals from the same type font as used for the large "4" and "8" surcharges. It could be concluded that both surcharges were applied by the Government Printing Office.

But the question remained: Why were the 4¢ stamps so scarce? Dr. Wood said this mystery was solved in 1937. Six copies of the stamp with the large red "4" had been discovered.

In 1937, a seventh copy was submitted to the Royal Philatelic Society of London by Commander N.E. Isemonger. In a letter to the society, Commander Isemonger explained that on behalf of his mother, he had sold the other six copies to W.H. Peckitt in 1911. The commander's father, Edwin E. Isemonger, was appointed postmaster general of the Straits Settlements in 1882 and served as colonial treasurer of the British colony from 1884 to 1886.

It seems that when the 8¢-on-12¢ stamps were surcharged with the large red "8," a few copies of the 4¢-on-5¢ also were surcharged with the large "4." The post office decided to surcharge all its 8¢-on-12¢ stamps with the large numeral, but not the remaining stock of the 4¢-on-5¢.

Dr. Wood said it seemed probable that the 4¢ surcharges were returned to the Straits Settlements Treasury. Apparently, Isemonger used them on his correspondence to his family, instead of destroying them. In doing so, he created some of the colony's greatest rarities.

Scott catalog prices these rarities at $15,000, although it incorrectly lists the price under the mint column. All copies are used. A copy was sold by Christie's/Robson Lowe in its March 11, 1987, auction as part of the Isleham collection sales. It realized $10,450, including a 10-percent buyer's premium.

Stockholm's Scarce Local

VALUE: $99,000

Only one tete-beche pair has been recorded of Sweden's 1-skilling-banco black local from Stockholm. The tete-beche pair was first recorded in 1970.

In an age when many collectors believe there are few rarities yet to be discovered, the uncovering of a major error more than a century after its issue is news. Yet, more than a decade passed between the discovery of a unique Swedish error and its making headlines in the philatelic press.

In 1970, an elderly gentleman asked the Boden Philatelic Society of Sweden to appraise a collection of Sweden he had inherited from a relative. Ake Eliasson, a member of the society and regional director of the Swedish Post Office, took on the task of evaluating the collection.

While sorting through the material, he discovered a pair of Sweden's 1856-62 1-skilling-banco black local. To his surprise, one of the stamps was upside down in relation to the other. Eliasson had discovered a previously unrecorded tete-beche error.

The black local stamp was first issued by the Swedish Post Office on July 1, 1856. It was intended to frank local letters and loose letters in Stockholm. Swedish collector Georg Menzinsky, in *Sweden Skilling Banco Stamps 1855-1858 and Local Stamps of 1856 and 1862*, said the black local stamp is the only real local stamp in the history of the Swedish postal service. It was in use until 1861.

The stamp carries no indication of value. From July 1, 1856, until July 1, 1858, it covered the 1sk rate. Beginning July 1, 1858, it covered the 3-ore rate.

Menzinsky said it is believed the stamp was engraved by Wilhelm Abraham Eurenius. Count Pehr Ambjorn Sparre printed the stamp. At first, Sparre produced the local with printing plates composed of 100 separate cliches. He later used plates manufactured in England composed of four quarter plates. The local features an ornamental design with the words "FRIMARKE/FOR/LOKALBREF" (Stamp for Local Letter).

Count Sparre apparently created the tete-beche error when he inserted one of the loose cliches upside down. Therefore, it is likely the error occurred in the first printing. The copy discovered by Eliasson is the only recorded example of this error.

The discovery of this rarity remained one of philately's best-kept secrets for more than a decade. Then, in 1986, the pair twice made headlines. The stamp realized 180,000 kronor (about $24,426) at the March 20-21, 1986, auction conducted by Postiljonen AB in Malmo, Sweden.

Later the same year, during the STOCKHOLMIA international stamp show, the error again was sold, this time by Frimarkshuset of Stockholm. The tete-beche pair opened at 300,000kr, and following tremendous activity was bid up to 575,000kr. When the bidding was over, Robert Markovits, a United States dealer, paid 661,000kr (about $99,000), including the 15-percent buyer's commission.

The tete-beche pair made the news twice in one year; yet, little still is known about the origins of this rarity.

In Search of Stars

VALUE: Indeterminable

Only known example of this Swiss 5-centime rayed-star postage due.

Switzerland's rarest stamp is a back-of-the book item — a postage due unknown to collectors until its discovery late in 1979.

Switzerland issued a series of postage-due stamps in 1878 using two designs. The first design consists of a numeral set against a background of rays surrounded by a circle of stars. The second features a numeral, but this time against a white background surrounded by a circle of stars.

The first design, with the rayed-star background, was used only for the 1-centime value — at least that is what collectors believed until 1979. That year, Heinz L. Katcher, a stamp dealer specializing in Switzerland, sat in his office sorting through an accumulation of Switzerland's first postage dues.

Katcher came across a postage-due stamp with the rayed-star background. At first glance, he thought it was the normal 1c value. A closer look, however, revealed that this was no ordinary postage due. The stamp had a 5c denomination, not a 1c.

Katcher's immediate reaction was to view the stamp with suspicion. Anyone familiar with Swiss stamps, as he certainly is, knew that the rayed-star background was used only for the 1c. Or was it? Was the 5c rayed-star variety a fake?

Katcher submitted his new discovery to rigorous tests and comparisons with other postage dues in the Swiss postal archives. The 5c rayed star passed the tests with flying colors. Collectors are uncertain how it occurred, but the stamp appears to be genuine.

In a 1980 issue of *The Swiss Philatelist*, Katcher speculates on how the error may have occurred. He says the stamps were printed in two separate processes — first the frames, then the value figure. The printer produced two sheets of 100 stamps from 250 cliches (50 cliches were spares).

During the printing, these cliches had to be removed and cleaned several times. Katcher says while the cliches were being cleaned, it is possible a 5c cliche accidently was inserted in place of the 1c. This is the most likely explanation; it means only a few copies of the error would have been produced. Since only one has been discovered in more than 100 years, it is reasonable to believe that few were printed. However, other possibilities do exist.

It is known that the printer experienced difficulties with the rayed-star background during the printing of the 1c, the first value of this set to be produced. He finally convinced the postal authorities to do away with the background, which is the reason the second design was used for the other values.

It is possible that an old rayed-star cliche found its way into the printing form while the 5c denominations were being printed. Or the printer may have used a discarded sheet of rayed-star frames without the values to experiment with the centering of the 5c. He also may have printed a few sheets of the 5c to prove that the rayed-star background was unsuitable, intending for these sheets to be destroyed.

It is unlikely collectors will ever know the reason the 5c rayed star was produced, but it is a rarity. The stamp carries a postmark of Bisseg, a town in the canton of Thurgau.

No additional copies of the stamp have been discovered. With only one in existence, it is difficult to establish a price. Katcher lists the stamp in his Amateur Collector's *Switzerland Catalogue*, but does not include a price. Since only one example exists, this postage due is by far the rarest of the Swiss issues.

Intentional or Unintentional?

VALUE: Indeterminable
The only example of the Swiss 1882-99 5-centime tete-beche pair in private hands. The other two examples are in the Swiss PTT Museum.

Most tete-beche pairs of Switzerland are relatively common. They were intentionally created in sheets intended for stamp booklets so the right-hand selvage could be used for stapling. Tete-beche pairs have one stamp in the normal upright position; the other stamp is inverted, or upside down, in relation to the normal stamp.

A glance at Scott catalog tells the collector that most Swiss tete-beche pairs command a premium over normal stamps, but this premium is slight when compared to prices for tete-beche pairs created in error. Scott catalog, however, lists one Swiss tete-beche pair which was a mistake. Only three examples of this pair have been recorded. They are among Switzerland's great rarities.

The stamp is the 5-centime maroon of the 1882-99 Numeral series. It was created when the printer accidentally inserted one cliche upside down. The Swiss PTT Museum in Bern owns two of the recorded tete-beche pairs — one mint and one used. For many years, these were the only genuine copies known to exist. Forgeries, on the other hand, were quite common.

Because of the numerous forgeries, when a 5c tete-beche pair came up for auction in 1958, many collectors assumed it to be another clever fake. Heinz Katcher, a dealer specializing in Swiss stamps, had a hunch the pair was genuine and submitted a bid.

He was successful in his bid. With the stamps in hand, Katcher was faced with the unenviable task of proving that they were a genuine tete-beche pair. Katcher says his pair was compared with those in the Swiss PTT Museum. Small breaks in the framelines, a blunted corner and other characteristics indicated that the pair was printed from the same cliches as the museum copies. Paper fibers and control marks further proved that the tete-beche pair was genuine.

Based on this evidence, the Swiss expert, Fritz Moser-Raz, issued a good expertizing certificate for the pair. But this was not the end. Katcher says it then was suspected that the faint postmark might be forged.

He enlisted the help of an expert on Swiss postmarks. With infrared photography the postmark was ''lifted'' from the stamp and examined carefully. The expert then studied and compared 80,000 Swiss postmarks. He concluded that Katcher's pair was genuinely used in Charmey-Bulle, Switzerland, January 1, 1888.

Based on this information, Moser-Raz issued another certificate proclaiming the pair to be a genuine used example of the rare tete-beche variety. The pair has since been sold to a Swiss collector. Although Scott catalog lists this rarity, it does not provide a price.

Stamp With No Value

VALUE: $16,500

*Trinidad's greatest rarity is this 1
penny of 1901 with the value omitted.*

The island of Trinidad in the West Indies is best known by stamp collectors for the Lady McLeod private issue. Trinidad's greatest rarity, however, is the 1901 1 penny with the value omitted. Although its story is not as romantic as the Lady McLeod's, the error is nonetheless one of the world's great rarities.

In the early 1900s, the Crown Agents, who were responsible for the postage stamps of many British colonies, requested a new color scheme for the stamps of several of its clients. The post offices in the colonies objected to the colors of current stamps, saying that they were ugly and did not conform to the requirements of the Washington Convention of the Universal Postal Union. Feeling that there were too many stamps of the same color, the UPU committee ruled that every stamp should have a distinctive color so it could be easily recognized.

The printer Thomas De La Rue in London, in response to Crown Agents' request, began using colored papers for the stamps of several British colonies, including Trinidad. Trinidad's 1901 1d stamp was printed in black on red. This value previously had been printed in lilac and rose. The design features a seated Britannia with "TRINIDAD" at the top and the value at the bottom. A single pane of 60 of the black-on-red stamp was discovered with the value inscription "ONE PENNY" omitted.

J.C. Lewis, who was the local postmaster in Trinidad at the time the stamp was issued, wrote in 1902 that seven examples of the missing-value stamps were sold before the error was discovered. He said four of the stamps were used on letters to Barbados; however, these covers have never been found. It is possible they were destroyed. Lewis, realizing the value of such errors, bought three copies and returned the remainder of the pane to London.

In his book, *The Royal Philatelic Collection*, Sir John Wilson, who was keeper of the collection, said 51 copies of the error were returned to London and destroyed. Only three examples have been recorded. All are mint.

One is in the Royal Collection in London, along with most of the rarities of the British Commonwealth. This copy was bought on behalf of King George V at a sale in London in 1914 to raise money for the Sailors' and Soldiers' Christmas Fund.

The second copy was sold by Robson Lowe November 18, 1959, for the descendants of the original owner. It realized £400. Christie's/Robson Lowe sold the third copy at auction on January 27, 1987. It realized £4,675 (about $7,000). This copy, with right margin, shows slight traces of the "NY" of "PENNY." According to the Christie's/Robson Lowe catalog, the stamp "almost certainly originally formed a pair" with the stamp sold in 1959.

The example sold in the January 1987 Christie's/Robson Lowe sale is accompanied by a 1902 letter from Bright and Son, London, to the postmaster at San Fernando, requesting examples of this variety. A note at the foot of the letter states, "Only 7 were sold four (4) of which were posted on letters and they were thoroughly inked over by the Postal authorities, consequently were of no use. J.C. Lewis Postmaster."

When added together, the 51 destroyed copies, the three known mint copies, and the four on letters to Barbados equal only 58. The pane consisted of 60 stamps. Robson Lowe says it is probable that two copies were retained in Trinidad for reference as has been the case with other rare West Indies stamps. Scott catalog lists the Trinidad missing-value error at $16,500.

An Impossible Position

VALUE: $63,250

The mystery position 11 of the Brattleboro provisional issue.

A mystery stamp exists among the Brattleboro, Vermont, postmaster's provisionals. Although this provisional issue was printed from a plate of 10 (two horizontal rows of five), a stamp from an 11th position exists.

The Brattleboro 5¢ was issued in 1846 by Postmaster Frederick N. Palmer. In the January 1869 *American Journal of Philately*, Palmer is quoted as saying his "object in issuing it was to accommodate the people and save myself labor in making and collecting quarterly bills, almost everything at that time being either charged or forwarded without prepayment."

He said, "I was disappointed in that effect, having still to charge the stamps and collect my bills."

Thomas Chubbuck of Brattleboro engraved the stamp. His imprint, "Eng'd by Thos. Chubbuck, Bratto.," appears below the middle stamp of the lower row (position 8). Chubbuck engraved each stamp separately, thus creating varieties which could be easily plated. Spaces about 1 millimeter wide divide the stamps. Thin lines of color were drawn through the middle of these spaces. These aid in the plating of the stamps.

The provisional was printed in black on buff wove paper. The design features the initials "Fnp" (Frederick N. Palmer) with

"BRATTLEBORO, VT" above and "5 CENTS" below. The letter "P." appears to the left; "O." to the right.

Palmer gave Chubbuck a sheet of eight as a souvenir. Chubbuck broke up the sheet and affixed the stamps to a scrapbook with red wax wafers. The stamps were canceled with red ink strokes in the upper left corner.

The mystery position 11 was discovered by Francis C. Foster. The stamp bears Chubbuck's red pen mark. But where did the stamp originate? In *The Postage Stamps of the United States*, John N. Luff said collectors have suggested that this stamp was engraved as a sample.

This rarity was once in the collection of Josiah K. Lilly, the pharmaceutical magnate. Robert A. Siegel Auction Galleries sold the stamp at its Rarities of the World sale April 5, 1986. It was sold, along with the Lapham-Colson complete reconstruction of the ten plate positions, for $63,250, including the 10-percent buyer's commission. Scott catalog lists the 5¢ Brattleboro provisional at $13,500 mint, $5,000 used, and $8,000 on cover.

En Route to Barcelona

VALUE: $70,000

This cover from New York to Barcelona, Spain, is the most outstanding of the covers bearing the scarce United States 1857-61 90¢ blue stamp.

A small printing edition and a short period of use contributed to the scarcity of the United States 90¢ stamp of the 1857-61 series. Genuine cancellations on this issue are rare. The stamp is extremely scarce on cover, with fewer than 10 recorded.

The U.S. Post Office Department issued the 90¢ blue high value in 1860. It features a handsome portrait of General George Washington in dress uniform. The portrait is taken from a painting by John Trumbull.

This stamp saw use particularly on covers to foreign destinations and on packages. The most spectacular cover bearing the 90¢ is addressed to Barcelona, Spain. The stamp is used with a 5¢ and 10¢ stamp. Stanley Ashbrook, one of the most distinguished philatelic scholars of this century, explained that since the U.S. had no postal treaty with Spain at that time, the cover went by American packet from New York to England, across the English Channel to Calais, then through France by French mail to Spain.

Financial wizard Alfred H. Caspary owned the cover until his death in 1955. In 1956, the cover realized $10,500 during the Caspary sales conducted by H.R. Harmer, Inc. Today, it is owned by Dr. Leonard Kapiloff.

Caspary also owned an unused block of 21 of the 90¢ deep blue. It sold for $10,100 in 1956. Another outstanding cover bears the 90¢ used with two 1¢ stamps, a 10¢ and 30¢ to make up the rate to the Cape of Good Hope. This item formerly was in the Saul Newbury collection. The Scott U.S. Specialized catalog lists the 90¢ stamp on cover at $70,000.

This 90¢ blue stamp was in use for only about a year. Since used copies are scarcer than mint, collectors should be alert to fake cancellations.

'𝒥' Before '𝓛'

VALUE: $8,500

The 10¢ "GOILAD" spelling error appears on this folded letter to Corpus Christie. This entire was in the Alfred Caspary and Josiah Lilly collections.

A spelling error on the Goliad, Texas, postmaster's provisional is one of the great rarities of the Confederate States of America. At the outset of the War Between the States, the governments of the North and South mutually agreed to discontinue postal services between the two sides. This policy went into effect May 31, 1861. No United States stamps were to be used by the Confederacy following this date.

This decision had a disastrous effect on the South. The Confederate Post Office Department found it impossible to produce stamps quickly enough. Confederate Postmaster General John H. Reagan ordered new stamps printed specially for the Confederacy, but these supplies would not arrive until October. During the interim, he advised his postmasters to get along as best they could.

Postmasters throughout the South began creating provisional stamps, envelopes and markings to meet their own needs. Some of these are attractive; others can best be described as crude. But the postmasters made the best of a bad situation and, in the process, created some of the true gems of philately.

In Goliad, Texas, Postmaster J.A. Clarke asked a local minister to print stamps for the town. The Reverend A.M. Cox of the Methodist church also owned the local newspaper, *The Messenger*, and thus had access to printing presses.

Cox set the type in two different fonts: italic and Roman capitals. Type I shows the inscription "Goliad/POSTAGE" in italics with the denomination (5¢ or 10¢) in the center. The second type shows the

VALUE: $15,000

The only recorded horizontal pair of the 5¢ Goliad provisional showing the "GOILAD" error (left) with a stamp showing the correct spelling.

same inscription but this time with "J.A. Clarke,/Post Master" on either side. Again the values are 5¢ and 10¢.

Both types feature a decorative border. When August Dietz published the *Dietz Specialized Catalog of the Postage Stamps of the Confederate States of America* in 1930, he quoted Fred Green, an authority on Texas locals, as saying: "The old newspaper and printing shop at Goliad is still doing business today. They still have the border that went around the Goliad local." Today, the border is housed in the Dietz Museum.

The stamps were printed on white wove or three different tinted papers — gray, pink and dark blue. In typesetting the second printing, Cox mistakenly transposed the letters "L" and "I" in "GOLIAD," resulting in the "GOILAD" spelling error.

This error occurred on both the 5¢ and 10¢. Singles of both are listed in the Scott U.S. Specialized at $5,500. Even normal copies of the Goliad provisional are scarce, cataloging between $4,500 and $5,000 for singles and as much as $7,500 on cover.

The famous British collector Thomas Keay Tapling owned an example of the type I 5¢ on gray paper on cover. The stamp is signed in manuscript "Clarke PM" in black, as is typical of all Goliad type I stamps.

The most spectacular item of the Goliad provisionals is the 5¢ spelling error printed se-tenant with a normal 5¢. Only one of these gems exist. It was owned by noted French collector Count Ferrari and was illustrated in the auction catalog when his collection was dispersed at the turn of the century. This horizontal pair shows the error at left. The pair is canceled with a light town postmark.

Alfred Caspary added this item to his extensive collection of Confederate provisionals. Caspary also owned normal copies of the provisionals as singles and on cover, and a copy of the 10¢ error on cover. The Scott U.S. Specialized catalog lists the 10¢ error on cover at $8,500.

Josiah K. Lilly paid $3,200 for the horizontal pair of 5¢ stamps, with the spelling error on the left stamp, when it was sold during the Caspary sales conducted by H.R. Harmer of New York in 1956. Today, Scott catalog lists the pair at $15,000.

The Innovative Postmaster

VALUE: $35,000

One of two known covers bearing the 1861 Grove Hill, Alabama, 5¢ postmaster's provisional stamp of the Confederate States of America.

Only two copies exist of the Confederate States of America Grove Hill 5¢ postmaster's provisional. Both are on cover and used in Alabama. The Grove Hill, Alabama, provisional stamp is a woodcut printed on white wove paper. In the *Confederate States Catalog*, August Dietz Sr. said the stamp apparently was handstamped.

By mutual agreement, postal services between the North and South were discontinued May 31, 1861, during the Civil War. No United States stamps were to be used for prepayment of postage in the South.

Since it was impossible for the Confederate Post Office Department to print stamps quickly enough to meet the need, Confederate Postmaster General John H. Reagan advised his postmasters to get along as best they could. A shortage of coins compounded the problem. Customers paid postmasters with Confederate States Treasury notes, but the postmasters often had no coins to make change.

Some Confederate postmasters improvised. They created their own provisional stamps and stamped envelopes. Most of these, including the Grove Hill 5¢, are crudely printed. Nevertheless, some are extremely valuable today. The Scott U.S. Specialized catalog lists the Grove Hill provisional at $35,000.

Alfred H. Caspary owned both covers bearing this provisional. In March 1956, when H.R. Harmer, Inc., auctioned Caspary's collection, one cover realized $7,000; the other $2,500. The more expensive cover bears a black town cancel and an attorney's return seal in red. It was owned by Count Ferrari and Arthur Hind before being purchased by Caspary. The other Grove Hill cover is canceled in pen in magenta.

Revived Stamped Envelope

VALUE: $6,500

Evidence recently uncovered suggests that the Tuscumbia provisional stamped envelope was issued in 1861, not 1858 as previously believed.

Most United States postmasters' provisionals were issued prior to the release of regular postage stamps by the U.S. Post Office Department. However, one provisional was issued by a postmaster more than 10 years after the first U.S. stamp was introduced.

For many years, collectors believed the Tuscumbia, Alabama, 3¢ postmaster's provisional stamped envelope was created by the postmaster in 1858 because of a shortage of stamps.

An 1855 Act of Congress made the use of stamps on mail compulsory. Collectors believed that in desperation, the postmaster of Tuscumbia created his own stamped envelope in 1858 to indicate prepayment of postage.

The Scott U.S. Specialized catalog has followed this belief. It lists the Tuscumbia provisional (12XU1) as being issued in 1858. In the Confederate States section, the Confederate Tuscumbia provisionals are listed as 84XU1-3. This follows the belief that the Tuscumbia stamped envelope was revived following the outbreak of the

Civil War in 1861. The postmaster of Tuscumbia simply reused the 1858 stamped envelope, replacing the "3" with a "5" or "10."

However, Patricia A. Kaufmann, a noted specialist collector of the Confederate States of America, presented evidence in 1984 that suggested that the Tuscumbia provisional was first issued in 1861, not 1858.

In an article in the September-October 1984 *Confederate Philatelist*, Kaufmann said the Tuscumbia provisional falls into a new category of provisionals, which are neither clearly U.S. nor Confederate. She said this new category consists of 3¢ provisionals issued by postmasters in states declaring allegiance to the Confederacy before the Confederate postal rates went into effect June 1, 1861.

The Confederacy was formed February 9, 1861. The Confederate postal service went into effect June 1 of that year, but stamps did not appear until mid-October. From June 1 until the issuance of Confederate stamps in October, many postmasters in southern states issued provisionals.

Kaufmann's study concludes that a different category of provisionals exists: those issued by postmasters in seceding states before the formation of the Confederate postal service.

The U.S. and the Confederate governments agreed that June 1 would be the start-up date of the Confederate postal service. Until then, according to Kaufmann's research, the Confederate government urged all southern postmasters to stay on the job and continue to remit funds to the U.S. Post Office Department. Postmasters in seceding states apparently were required to take a loyalty oath. Most did. Those who didn't were denied U.S. postage stamps.

During this brief period, from the formation of the Confederacy to the establishment of the Confederate postal service, U.S. stamps and U.S. postal rates were still valid in the seceding states. But, for some reason, a few southern postmasters found themselves without stamps. Kaufmann said a few of these desperate postmasters issued provisionals, not in the 5¢ and 10¢ denominations generally encountered on Confederate or early U.S. provisionals, but in a 3¢ denomination to meet the U.S. domestic postal rate.

The Tuscumbia postmaster issued a crude buff colored envelope, featuring a simple red circular handstamp with "Tuscumbia, Ala." within a circle. A straightline "PAID" was below the value, a numeral "3." The handstamp was applied in black to the upper right corner of the envelope. Used covers also bear the circular postmark of Tuscumbia.

The provisional envelope was first discovered by collectors in 1912. Two copies were found in the Carroll-Hoy correspondence. Kaufmann said the Carroll-Hoy correspondence is often helpful in dating Confederate items because this firm had been known as Buchanan, Carroll and Company prior to being known as Carroll, Hoy and Company. The change in the name appears to have taken place in approximately mid-1858, according to Kaufmann.

Since the two Tuscumbia covers were dated in April and May, the year date could not have been 1858, explained Kaufmann. It must have been 1859, 1860 or 1861. "Logic dictates that the year date should be 1861," Kaufmann said.

Fewer than a half dozen examples of this provisional exists. The small number of covers bearing the U.S. 3¢ stamp of 1857 used in Tuscumbia has been cited by some collectors as proof that this stamped envelope was issued because of a shortage of stamps. Kaufmann, however, believes this means nothing, as there are numerous 3¢ 1857 issues known used in the Confederate period. "It simply shows that the postmaster, who had been using the 3¢ Tuscumbia provisional, was able to obtain a supply of U.S. stamps in May of 1861," Kaufmann explained.

Renowned collector Alfred Caspary owned an example of the provisional and also a cover bearing the 3¢ 1857 stamp affixed over the provisional handstamp and tied by a black "TUSCUMBIA, Ala., May 20" postmark. Both rarities were formerly in the Storow and Colonel Green collections.

The provisional realized $1,600 in the Caspary sales conducted by H.R. Harmer, Inc., in 1955. The cover bearing the 3¢ 1857 on the provisional handstamp realized $750.

Scott catalog lists the 3¢ provisional at $6,500. The 5¢ and 10¢ envelopes are priced from $550 to $1,100.

Cycling the Mail

VALUE: $1,500

This No. 42 cover shows the first design of the Bicycle stamp with the spelling error "SAN FRANSISCO," instead of "SAN FRANCISCO."

A railway strike and a fad combined to inspire one of the most inventive means of transporting mail ever used in the United States. The movement of mail screeched to a halt in some parts of the country during the Pullman strike in 1894. California was particularly affected by the strike.

Entrepreneur Arthur Banta decided to take advantage of a fad that was sweeping the country. Everyone was bicycling in the 1890s. Bicycle clubs met regularly; races became a major sporting event. Banta, owner of a bicycle shop in Fresno, California, decided to further capitalize on the bicycle industry by establishing a mail service to move the mail during the strike. Actually, John C. Nourse, a Fresno grocer, came up with the idea. He suggested it to Banta.

When Eugene Donze, a local engraver and stamp collector, heard of the proposed service, he suggested to Banta that stamps be issued. Banta agreed, and Donze created the stamps. They were printed in Fresno by the Commercial Printing Company.

The stamps were diamond-shaped. They were printed directly from a die, one at a time, to form sheets of six. The design features a cyclist riding along a roadway with a mountainous landscape in the background. At the top of the stamp are the initials "A.R.U." (American Railway Union) and at the bottom, "STRIKE."

The first die engraved by Donze contained a spelling error. The inscription read, "FRESNO AND SAN FRANSISCO/BICYCLE MAIL ROUTE." Note the misspelling of Francisco. This spelling error was detected shortly after the stamps came into use. Donze corrected the die by re-engraving a "C" over the "S." He also added his initials, "ED," to the die.

In his book, *The Fresno and San Francisco Bicycle Mail of 1894* (published by Leonard H. Hartmann in 1982), Lowell B. Cooper says he knows of only four full sheets of the Bicycle stamps from the first printing showing the spelling error.

The Fresno and San Francisco Bicycle Mail Service began carrying mail July 7, 1894. The service used eight relays to cover the distance of 210 miles between Fresno and San Francisco in 18 hours. A fee of 25¢ was charged for each letter. Letters were franked with regular U.S. stamps, as well as the Bicycle stamps, which met with the approval of the U.S. Post Office Department.

A few covers were carried on the first days of the service without the Bicycle stamp. The earliest known cover bears a pictorial bicycle handstamp dated July 7, 1894. The cover is addressed to Oakland, California. It also carries the registration number 4.

Covers originating from Fresno were numbered, and the number was registered in a book. However, Cooper says collectors have been unable to find this book. The No. 4 cover is franked with a 2¢ U.S. stamp and the Bicycle stamp with the corrected spelling. The U.S. stamp is tied by a July 9 Oakland postmark, so it is likely the cover was carried on the July 8 run.

A cover with registration No. 42 bears a copy of the first printing of the Bicycle stamp showing the spelling error. Cooper says this is the first cover he has seen bearing the return mail handstamp, "Answer may be left with OVERMAN WHEEL CO. Larkin & McAllister St., S.F. THROUGH SERVICE DAILY." Overman Wheel Company was the northern terminal of the service in San Francisco. The No. 42 cover realized about $1,500 in a Daniel Kelleher sale in 1981.

Donze engraved a second die. Cooper says it appears this die was used only for printing stamped envelopes. He says he knows of only three examples of die II. Each is on the size 4½ white 1890 Plimpton stamped envelope. Cooper estimates that a dozen covers may exist with this die.

Die II also shows the corrected spelling. It can be distinguished from the recut die by the scratches on the roadway behind the cyclist. The scratches run upwards to the right. Also, the white valley under the last "N" of "SAN FRANCISCO" is almost vertical, unlike the recut die.

For some unknown reason, die II was retired from service shortly after it was first used. The recut die was used for the majority of the stamped envelopes.

Numbered covers actually carried over the bicycle route are scarce. Scott catalog prices covers from $850 to $1,350. However, they could conceivably sell for higher prices. Robert A. Siegel Auction Galleries sold two Bicycle Mail covers in its December 16-18, 1986, auction for $770 and $1,815, each including 10-percent buyer's premium. Unused and used stamps are fairly common. Cooper estimates that about 380 non-philatelic and 200 philatelic covers were prepared. Only about 150 exist today. Of these, about 80 percent are philatelic, he says. More than half the 40 stamped envelopes produced are in collections today. Others may still exist.

By July 15, the railway strike had ended, and normal mail service had resumed. The bicycle mail service made its last run July 19, drawing to a close this unusual method of moving the mail. In a period of just 12 days, some of philately's most interesting covers were created.

A counterfeit die of the Bicycle stamp has been recorded. It is defaced by one heavy horizontal cut and five vertical cuts. It exists on cover. Defaced stamps also were created for a 1935 memorial run of the bicycle service, celebrating the 40th anniversary of its inauguration.

𝒩otches and ℋoles

VALUE: $41,400

A horizontal strip of three of the U.S. 4¢ brown Grant issue with Scher-mack private perforations franks this registered cover sent to Germany.

Collectors are baffled the first time they see a stamp with those peculiar slotted perforations known as Schermack perfs. For the most part, stamps with these odd notches and holes are common. But there is one exception — the United States 1906-08 4¢ brown, known as Scott 314A.

This stamp was issued imperforate in April 1908. All copies were intended for use in the Schermack stamp-dispensing machines. The Schermack Mailing Machine Company of Detroit, along with a few other companies, pioneered stamp-vending machines in the United States. The U.S. Post Office Department sold these compa-nies sheets of imperforate stamps to be made into coils for their stamp-vending machines.

The companies then created their own perforation devices. Schermack's perforations are the most famous of all. Several types exist — from notches and slots to various sizes of holes.

According to Max Johl's *United States Postage Stamps 1902-1935*, Schermack received a request in 1908 from two Detroit companies, Burroughs Adding Machine Company and Hamilton Carbadt Company. The companies needed 4¢ coils to meet the postal rate for mailing catalogs. Prior to this, Schermack machines had offered only 1¢ or 2¢ stamps.

Schermack ordered 10,000 4¢ stamps from the U.S. Post Office Department to fulfill its customers' needs.

The Post Office Department sent a request to the Bureau of Engraving and Printing for imperforate sheets of a 4¢ stamp showing a portrait of General Ulysses S. Grant. Since one of the binder-

VALUE: $17,500

This U.S. 4¢ stamp is an example of type III of the Schermack perforations.

ies for the companies owned a Schermack machine, the stamps were sent directly to the bindery.

Karl Koslowski stopped in at the bindery one day to chat with friends. The sheets of imperforate stamps intrigued Koslowski, who collected stamps. He leafed through the sheets to satisfy his curiosity. One of his friends at the bindery even offered to sell him a sheet, but Koslowski declined the offer.

Sitting at home that evening, Koslowski began thinking about the stamps. He had second thoughts about declining his friend's offer. Maybe he would like to have a sheet of imperforates for his collection. Early the next morning, he returned to the bindery to tell his friend he had reconsidered the offer and would buy one sheet.

However, he was too late. The stamps already had been perforated with the Schermack type III perforations consisting of vertical notches between the stamps. These were even more attractive to Koslowski than the imperforates. He purchased 50 of the perforated stamps for $2. He used 35 on correspondence to friends around the world, unaware that these stamps someday would become rarities.

Fewer than 40 copies of this stamp exist today. Scott catalog lists them at $17,500 mint and $9,000 used. On cover, the stamp is priced at $22,500. Only two covers exist. Joseph Agris, a collector in Texas, owns both. One of these covers was auctioned in New York City November 19-23, 1985, by David Feldman. This 1908 registered cover, from Koslowski to a friend in Germany, is franked with a horizontal strip of three of the 4¢ brown with Schermack perfs. It also carries a 1¢ Jamestown stamp and a purple Detroit, Michigan, circular datestamp.

Feldman describes this as "the rarest 20th century U.S. cover in existence." Agris bought it at the November 1985 sale for $41,400, including a 15-percent buyer's commission.

The second cover bears a single of the 4¢ tied by a Sicklerville, New Jersey, postmark dated April 8, 1909. This cover is addressed to Koslowski.

Robert A. Siegel Auction Galleries sold a single at its May 25, 1986, AMERIPEX auction for $14,850. John Kaufmann sold a pair at his December 7, 1985, auction for $49,500. Both prices include the 10-percent buyer's premium.

Bluish Paper Scandal

VALUE: $14,000 each

Bribery of a postal official and embezzlement resulted in the release of the United States scarce 4¢ and 8¢ bluish paper printings of 1909.

An experiment, embezzlement and bribery combine to make the 1909 4¢ and 8¢ bluish paper stamps two of the most intriguing stamps in United States philately. Max G. Johl, in *United States Postage Stamps 1902-1935*, referred to these stamps as "the rarest 'non-error' stamps of the twentieth century."

For many years, collectors believed the bluish paper stamps were part of an experiment to minimize the shrinkage of the paper when it was dampened prior to the intaglio printing. Herman Herst Jr., however, dispelled this theory. He said the stamps were part of an experiment to prevent the tendency of the stamps to curl up. This was a constant complaint of postal clerks.

The Bureau of Engraving and Printing experimented by adding 30-percent rag to the paper pulp. This gave the paper a bluish tint. Quantities of the 1¢ and 2¢ Washington-Franklins and the 2¢ Lincoln commemorative were printed on this bluish paper. These stamps were distributed to post offices in the Washington, D.C., area along with the normal issues.

Since A.L. Lawshe, third assistant postmaster general, frequently was absent due to illness, his assistant, Arthur M. Travers, took over many of Lawshe's duties at that time. During a visit to the BEP, Travers was informed of the bluish paper experiment by Joseph E. Ralph, director of the Bureau.

Not one to pass up an opportunity, Travers suggested that the Bureau print additional values — 3¢ through $1 — on the remaining bluish-paper stock. He asked that they be printed immediately, before the plates began to show signs of wear.

Ralph pointed out that there was no need to rush the printing of the 50¢ and $1 since these values seldom went to press. It would be some time before the plates began to show signs of wear.

According to *Sloane's Column* by George B. Sloane, the Bureau printed 4,000 each of the 3¢, 5¢, 8¢, 10¢, 13¢ and 15¢ denominations; 4,400 of the 4¢; and 5,200 6¢. Travers' ordered the delivery of these stamps to the curator of the U.S. Postal Museum, the U.S. Post Office Department's official files and, of course, to the office of the third assistant postmaster general, where he was in charge. Each office was to receive 100 sets. Another 100 sets were to be retained for surplus.

Travers ordered the remainder of the printing destroyed. But a mix-up occurred at the BEP. The remaining supply was not destroyed but was incorporated into the stock of regular stamps and distributed to post offices. These sheets of experimental stamps could be identified by a manuscript "X" in the sheet margins.

It was not long before collectors discovered these stamps at their local post offices and through their favorite stamp dealer. They began compiling sets. However, in each case the 4¢ and 8¢ values were missing. These denominations simply were not available through the post offices nor through normal philatelic channels.

This set the stage for Joseph A. Steinmetz, a prominent Philadelphia collector and dealer. Dr. Stanley M. Bierman detailed the life of this controversial figure in the February 1987 *The Chronicle of the U.S. Classic Postal Issues*, the journal of the U.S. Philatelic Classics Society. Steinmetz had strong political ties in Washington. After learning of the existence of the 4¢ and 8¢ bluish paper printings, Steinmetz contacted Travers. He offered Travers a bribe of $1,500 for the elusive stamps.

Herman Herst Jr. tells the story in *Nassau Street*. Travers agreed to meet Steinmetz at a Washington post office where the 4¢ and 8¢ blue paper panes, along with a set of the other values, were exchanged. The panes were placed on top of the pile when Steinmetz came to the counter to purchase them. Travers replaced the pilfered stock with regular U.S. 1908 printings.

Steinmetz succeeded in cornering the market on the 4¢ and 8¢ but also raised the ire of fellow stamp dealers by bragging about his acquisition. Particularly annoyed was Philip H. Ward Jr. Steinmetz offered to sell Ward copies of the elusive stamps, but Ward refused to pay the price.

Ward soon discovered that the stamps could not be obtained through normal philatelic channels. Furious that Steinmetz had duped fellow dealers by cornering the market by underhanded methods, Ward demanded an investigation by postal authorities.

According to Herst, a check of Travers' long-distance telephone calls revealed several calls to and from Steinmetz. Following a full investigation, Travers was arrested and charged with violating postal laws, embezzlement and conspiracy to perform illegal acts with Steinmetz. He pleaded guilty and was fined $1,500.

Steinmetz also was indicted and convicted on conspiracy charges. He was scheduled to go to jail, but once again he pulled political strings. Herst said that during the re-election campaign of William Howard Taft, the president was asked to act in Steinmetz' behalf. One word from the president, and Steinmetz was free, bringing down the curtain on one of philately's biggest scandals. The conviction, however, stood.

For his efforts in the investigation, Ward supposedly received a block of each of the 4¢ and 8¢ on bluish paper. Collectors continue to seek the 4¢ and 8¢ stamps today. An indication of their scarcity is their catalog value. The Scott U.S. Specialized lists the stamps at $14,000 each.

Half-Millimeter Difference

VALUE: $17,600

*Few copies exist of this 1923 2¢
Harding Memorial perf 11 stamp.*

Public demand resulted in four types of the United States 1923 2¢ Harding Memorial issue, one of which is a great rarity.

President Warren G. Harding died in San Francisco August 2, 1923, following a short illness. In less than a month, the U.S. Post Office Department had a 2¢ memorial stamp printed and issued. The stamp made its debut September 1, 1923, at Marion, Ohio, Harding's birthplace.

But it was not only the quickness with which it was issued that made this stamp exceptional. Many other factors set it apart from previous U.S. issues.

For the Harding Memorial issue, the U.S. Post Office Department waived the Universal Postal Union regulation requiring the domestic letter rate stamp of all countries to be printed in red. The Harding stamp was printed in black. This issue was the first commemorative to be issued in two types of printing — flatbed press and rotary press. Also, more stamps were printed for this issue than any commemorative preceding it.

The unprecedented popularity of this stamp resulted in the two types of printing. The flatbed presses could not print stamps quickly enough to meet the demand. The Bureau of Engraving and Printing began using its rotary presses for this issue. Prior to this, no U.S. stamp above the 1¢ denomination had been printed on the rotary press.

The 2¢ Harding Memorial rotary stamps went on sale September 12. The flatbed printings were perforated 11; the rotary perf 10. At least that is what collectors believed for several years after the stamps were issued. However, 15 years later the 1¢ denomination of the 1923 rotary printed definitive series was discovered perf 11.

Collectors suspected that the 2¢ Harding Memorial rotary printing might also exist perf 11. Their suspicions soon were confirmed. The 2¢ memorial stamp did indeed exist perf 11 on the rotary printing as well as the flatbed printing. But only a small quantity of the perf 11 rotary printings have been discovered. None is known mint. In 1982, the Philatelic Foundation reported that it certified only 39 of the 134 Harding Memorial rotary printings submitted between 1945 and 1982.

The rotary stamp is taller than the flatbed printing. The rotary perf 11 measures 19¼ millimeters wide by 22½ to 22¾mm wide; the flat is 19¼mm by 22¼mm. That half a millimeter means the difference between a stamp which is listed in Scott catalog at 10¢ and one that is priced at $13,500.

Two rotary printed perf 11 stamps were auctioned in 1986 during the AMERIPEX international stamp show in Chicago. On May 25, during the show, Robert A. Siegel Auction Galleries sold a copy on piece for $12,650, including a 10-percent buyer's premium. Steve Ivy sold a copy the next day for $17,600, including a 10-percent buyer's premium. Ivy sold another copy at its August 22-24, 1986, auction for $17,050, including the 10-percent buyer's premium.

Public demand for the 2¢ Harding Memorial also convinced the U.S. Post Office Department to issue another type — an imperforate version suitable for framing by collectors. These stamps are common. Scott lists them at $13 mint and $6 used.

The Lilac Swan

VALUE: $2,640
This full-sheet-margin copy of the Western Australia 2-penny lilac color error was in the Caspary collection.

Western Australia's most famous error is the inverted frame on the 1854-57 4-penny blue, also incorrectly referred to as the "inverted swan." But Western Australia also has another scarce error, although it is often overshadowed by the more-famous 4d invert.

While the invert is listed in Scott catalog at $100,000, its neglected cousin, the 2-penny lilac error of color, is listed at $13,500 mint and $5,500 used, a mere fraction of the value of the invert. Yet, the error of color is appearing on the market more frequently. Examples of this error were offered for sale twice during 1987.

In 1862, Crown Agents, the philatelic representative for Western Australia, awarded the contract for Western Australia's stamps to Thomas De La Rue and Company in England. Perkins, Bacon, who previously had printed the colony's stamps, handed over the plates to Crown Agents, which subsequently gave these to De La Rue. De La Rue was not accustomed to the recess (engraved) printing process, and a few problems arose, particularly in the form of color varieties. For example, the 6d violet is found in shades of lilac and red-lilac.

During the printing of the 6d in 1879, Western Australia's second major error was created. The 2d, which normally was printed in yellow, was produced in the lilac shade of the 6d.

Count Ferrari, one of the world's most famous stamp collectors, owned a copy of the 2d lilac error of color. Alfred Caspary, one of the great collectors of the 20th century, owned one of the finest examples of this error — a copy with a full sheet margin at left. When H.R. Harmer Ltd. of England sold the Caspary collection in 1958, the stamp realized £130.

The British stamp dealer, Stanley Gibbons, obtained several copies of the error from the postmaster at Albany, Western Australia. In the April 1930 *Collectors Club Philatelist*, Charles J. Phillips told how the postmaster, "in a letter enclosing £20 worth of unused values, remarked that he had taken the liberty of sending half a sheet (120) of 2d printed in the color of the 6d . . ." Phillips said the postmaster "apologized for charging the last named price, as he had been charged that by the authorities."

Gibbons was charged 5 shillings each for the errors. At his March 7-8, 1987, auction, Greg Manning sold what was described as a faulty example of this rarity for $1,650, including the 10-percent buyer's premium. As part of the Isleham Collection sales, Christie's/Robson Lowe sold another copy of the error during its March 11, 1987, auction. It realized $2,640, including the 10-percent buyer's premium.